"Mark Jones writes books that expose the ~~trendy lies of our day and counters~~ ers them with sound Reformed theology and eternal scriptural truths. One of those trendy lies declares that faith deconstruction is authentic, mature, and safe—but nothing could be further from the truth. Reading Dr. Jones's *The Pilgrim's Regress* is like getting the right prescription eyeglasses and finally seeing what is before our eyes. Dr. Jones carefully and faithfully takes the reader through the dangerous stages of backsliding and the horror of apostasy. Each chapter is a wake-up call providing clear spiritual medicine for Christians to progress and not regress in their faith. I cannot recommend this book highly enough. It's a must-read."
—**Rosaria Butterfield**, author, *Five Lies of Our Anti-Christian Age*

"Warning! Don't read this book if you don't want to be confronted with the danger of backsliding to which every Christian is constantly exposed. Warning! Don't read this book if you don't want to be encouraged by learning of the resources readily available to every Christian for countering the ever-present tendency to backsliding. Reading this book has been a searching experience for me personally, as Mark Jones carefully delineates the various regressive tendencies that plague the Christian life, explores the difference between them and irremediable apostasy, and unfolds in a deeply probing way the thoroughly sufficient and efficacious remedies that Scripture provides. Don't heed my warnings. Read this book!"
—**Richard B. Gaffin Jr.**, Professor of Biblical and Systematic Theology, Emeritus, Westminster Theological Seminary

"Few address the subject of this book, yet backsliding and apostasy are genuine realities in the story of the church. This fresh study of the subject not only examines the nature of backsliding but also, in John Owen–like fashion, probes deeply into its sources. As my favorite Christian author, Andrew Fuller, once noted in a famous tract on the backslider, the abandonment of evangelical truth does not take place out of the blue. It is usually preceded by a serious neglect of 'all close walking with God.' Sadly, this is a much-needed tract for our crooked age. Thankfully, though, it provides a robust gospel remedy for this ill that ails so many of our churches."
—**Michael A. G. Azad Haykin**, Professor of Church History, The Southern Baptist Theological Seminary

"Learning is like rowing upstream: a lack of progress is tantamount to regress. This admonition from the *Analects of Confucius* is common sense. But as the late J. I. Packer used to say: "Common sense is a Christian virtue. The Bible calls it wisdom." Christians who toy with the idea that we can bet on our having been saved in Christ—having been given more than just a 'taste' of 'the heavenly gift' (Heb. 6:4–6)—without making spiritual progress are in a way more foolish than pagans who still consult common sense and experience. Drawing on a wealth of Christian wisdom from ages past, Mark Jones takes us on a journey through biblical admonitions against backsliding, reminding us of the 'strong encouragement to hold fast to the hope set before us' (v. 18). In a culture now beginning to be wearied by the hypocrisy of so-called positive energies, a culture that in turn proposes to embrace the 'true self' by giving in to the downward stream of turning from God, this refreshing book reminds us of a genuinely Christian way of being authentic as sinners saved by grace."
—**Shao Kai Tseng**, Research Professor in the School of Philosophy, Zhejiang University

"Dr. Mark Jones's *The Pilgrim's Regress: Guarding against Backsliding and Apostasy in the Christian Life* is a masterly exploration of the complex spiritual journey that every believer undertakes. With eloquent prose and an unwavering commitment to biblical truth, Jones weaves a tapestry of profound theological insight, pastoral wisdom, and genuine compassion that speaks to the heart of every Christian pilgrim on his or her path to consummated glory. Delving into the intricate dynamics of the Christian walk, he unravels the mysteries of grace, perseverance, and the relentless battle against indwelling sin. His profound insights and practical solutions offer guidance to believers of all backgrounds. This literary masterpiece is a beacon of understanding, providing solace, wisdom, and hope for every follower of Christ. This is a must-read for all believers."
—**Christopher Yuan**, speaker, author of *Holy Sexuality and the Gospel*, and producer of *The Holy Sexuality Project* video series for parents and their teens

The Pilgrim's Regress

The Pilgrim's Regress

Guarding against Backsliding and
Apostasy in the Christian Life

Mark Jones

P&R
PUBLISHING
P.O. BOX 817 • PHILLIPSBURG • NEW JERSEY 08865-0817

Unless otherwise indicated, Scripture quotations are from the ESV® Bible (The Holy Bible, English Standard Version®), copyright © 2001 by Crossway, a publishing ministry of Good News Publishers. Used by permission. All rights reserved.

Scripture quotations marked (KJV) are from the Holy Bible, King James Version (Authorized Version). First published in 1611.

Printed in the United States of America

ISBN: 978-1-62995-966-5 (pbk)
ISBN: 978-1-62995-967-2 (ePub)

Library of Congress Cataloging-in-Publication Data has been applied for.

With appreciation to two faithful pastors in my early Christian
life who helped this pilgrim to progress:

Leigh Robinson

Jack C. Whytock

*Now to him who is able to keep you from stumbling and to present
you blameless before the presence of his glory with great joy, to the
only God, our Savior, through Jesus Christ our Lord, be glory, majesty,
dominion, and authority, before all time and now and forever. Amen.*
Jude 24-25

Contents

Foreword

Every Christian has witnessed a brother or sister in the Lord drifting from the faith that he or she once possessed. We have all witnessed some who were once committed and zealous growing cold, growing distant, growing dissatisfied. Alarmed, we wonder: Are they backsliding or are they in the process of rejecting the Christian faith altogether? Though we have all seen this, few of us have read good books about it. Though the experience is so common, resources are few. And for that reason I'm thankful for *The Pilgrim's Regress*. This book meets a need and fills a void.

In *The Pilgrim's Regress*, Mark Jones has written about a topic that is both alarming and comforting. It is alarming in its diagnosis of a spiritual condition that can afflict any of us if we fail to keep watch, if we fail to stay true, if we fail to remain faithful. Until our race is complete and we are safely in heaven, not one of us can stay still, not one of us can coast, not one of us can rest on our laurels. This book alarms and sobers us with the fear of what may befall us if we do not remain obedient to God and committed to his means of grace.

But this book is also comforting because it assures us that our God loves those who are truly his and that he will not let even one be lost. It assures us that none of us has sinned beyond the reach of his grace or beyond his capacity to forgive. It assures us that God is always eager and willing to receive us back, even when we have drifted so much and slid so far.

Whether you are attempting to understand and guide someone who seems to be walking away, whether you are a pastor wondering whether one of your parishioners is backslidden or fallen away, or whether you have concerns for the state of your own soul, *The Pilgrim's Regress* will bless and help you. Drawing from the deep wells of Christians from ages long past, and fully dependent on the Bible, Jones writes with a theologian's precision and a pastor's love. He writes to encourage and to comfort, to reprove and to exhort. He writes ultimately to glorify our God and serve his people.

Tim Challies
www.challies.com

Preface

In 2013 I wrote *Antinomianism: Reformed Theology's Unwelcome Guest?* (P&R Publishing). It addressed several problems occurring in broadly Reformed circles. At the time, an idea emerged that sanctification was the art of *simply* getting used to one's justification. Usually associated with this belief were other worrying views that became entrenched in much popular thinking. Several shibboleths emerged that were not quite in line with historic Reformed orthodoxy, but to query them was to put oneself at risk of being "anti-gospel." To warn believers of potential spiritual harm because of spiritual lukewarmness seemed to be contrary to the frequent calls to believers to "rest in God's amazing grace."

We can be thankful for Christian books that faithfully speak of the glories of God's salvation through Christ. But what about books that address issues that are a little uncomfortable for us to consider? Are we so naive as to think that all is well in the church today? And if we agree that some serious problems plague the church, are we prepared to accept that sometimes we need to be exhorted and warned, not just encouraged?

This book looks at Christian backsliding and, to a lesser extent, apostasy. To teach and preach on backsliding, one must have clear ideas of what is required to walk faithfully with God. Since many wish to make the Christian life merely a matter of resting in God's grace, they don't feel too comfortable talking about the reality that one can backslide, even while in a state of grace, and suffer some spiritual harm (e.g., infrequent communion with God). But difficult topics are not to be avoided. They require care, precision, and a pastoral aim to help God's people. So in this book on backsliding and apostasy, I have enlisted the help of pastors and theologians from various eras in church history who found it necessary to write on these issues. A topic that seems to be avoided today certainly was not in past eras.

Some of these guides include the so-called Puritans, though I prefer to think of most of these British theologians as Reformed catholics. After all, their sermons and writings are littered with references to many pastors and theologians from previous eras of church history (hence, catholicity), but they also were part of a robust Reformed and ecumenical confessional tradition in one way or another (hence, Reformed). The Puritans are not always well liked, even in certain Reformed circles. This is odd for a few reasons, not least of which is the possibly bothersome fact that the Puritans wrote the confessional documents that many Presbyterian churches embrace to this day. Be that as it may, many will speak of how the Puritans rob one of assurance, and they may point to John Owen's work on mortification or even John Bunyan's *The Pilgrim's Progress* as examples. Yet it is Thomas Goodwin's work *The Heart of Christ in Heaven towards Sinners on Earth* that provided the backbone to Dane Ortlund's well-received book *Gentle and Lowly*.

One must wonder whether these critics of the Puritans have read widely and carefully in other eras of church history. If such people have reservations about Puritan pastoral theology, I cannot imagine how they would feel after reading many of the early church fathers or the medieval theologians. Even first-generation Reformers wrote some startling things that would make us squirm a little. And whatever you do, do not read the chapter "Remember Lot's Wife" in J. C. Ryle's book *Holiness*.

In this book, while I made use of the Puritans, I also enjoyed very much the work of theologians from diverse traditions such as Thomas Boston (1676–1732), Andrew Fuller (1754–1815), Archibald Alexander (1772–1851), and Octavius Winslow (1808–78). None of these men were Puritans. But they wrote clearly and perceptively on backsliding and apostasy. They understood the dangers of backsliding, its symptoms, and the cures required to bring saints back into close fellowship with God and his people.

This is not an academic work, but a book on pastoral theology. Ordinarily, pastors should be best suited to write and preach on this topic, given that they have had direct dealings with backsliders and apostates. This is a sad reality that pastors face, regardless of the health of their churches. I am deeply thankful for the faithfulness of God's servants in my own church, where I have been privileged to minister for over fifteen years. During this time, some have drifted and returned; some have drifted and, sadly, not (yet?) returned; some are apparently drifting; others may yet drift; and many are gloriously growing in grace as they walk toward glory. In truth, the backsliding of church members is only part of the story. In keeping with one of the messages of this book, I also don't know how often God has used my fellowship with these faithful saints to preserve me (and them) from backsliding. But I do know enough by now to thank God for them with this in mind.

Of all the books that I have been able to write, this one has been particularly difficult, not only because it hits close to home concerning many people in my own life whom I love, but also because I know my own heart, and some of the writing on these pages came naturally based on personal (and painful) experience. For that reason, I pray that if there is hurt on these pages for you, there will also be hope, healing, and happiness.

Acknowledgments

Writing this book has been made possible by the help of many people. In particular, I would like to thank John Hughes at P&R Publishing for all the work he has done in making this book a reality. Also, good editors are hard to find, but Karen Magnuson is one such editor. My friend Bob McKelvey read through the entire manuscript and made many helpful comments. He has been a great blessing to me over the years since he first supervised my MA thesis on John Owen. In Vancouver, I am blessed to have a supportive congregation with elders who encourage me to write for the wider church. And in this instance, a deacon at Faith Church, Mike O'Donaghue, read through the manuscript and offered some specific encouragements. Finally, I could not ask for a better family. My wife and children are, to quote Tina Turner, simply the best. *Soli Deo Gloria.*

see p 5

1) What is backsliding? (xviii)
2) What is apostasy? (xxii)
3) Compare and contrast. (xxi/xxii)
4) What's the point of this book? (xxii)

Introduction

There is no such thing in the New Testament as a believer whose perseverance is so guaranteed that he can afford to ignore the warning notes which are sounded so frequently. (Sinclair Ferguson)[1]

The great nineteenth-century Presbyterian theologian William Plumer tells of someone accusing a minister of opposing the doctrine of the perseverance of the saints. The minister affirmed that he was in fact against the perseverance of (unrepentant) sinners, while fully supportive of the perseverance of the saints. Not satisfied with that, the accuser replied, "Do you think that a child of God cannot fall very low, and yet be restored?"[2] Without denying the possibility, the minister calmly remarked that it would be "very dangerous to make the experiment."[3] Plumer agrees and adds, "He who is determined to see how far he may

1. Sinclair Ferguson, *The Christian Life: A Doctrinal Introduction* (Edinburgh: Banner of Truth, 1981), 174.
2. William S. Plumer, *Vital Godliness: A Treatise on Experimental and Practical Piety* (New York: American Tract Society, 1864), 148.
3. Plumer, 148.

decline in religion and yet be restored, will lose his soul."[4] While
I might prefer to say "will likely lose his soul," Plumer's instinct
appears correct: it is a dangerous thing to willfully drift away
from God, otherwise known as Christian backsliding.

Christians generally accept the plain teaching of the Scriptures
that, once in Christ, they are to become like him in holiness (Rom.
8:29), as they die unto sin and live unto righteousness. The life
of faith (Gal. 2:20)—the sanctified life—is a journey "from one
degree of glory to another" (2 Cor. 3:18). But Christians also
realize that remaining, indwelling sin keeps us from pursuing
Christ as we should and, worse yet, sometimes leads us to pull
away from him. Such a drift, left unchecked, we call *backsliding*.

A pull away from living well for God, and by God's grace,
seems a constant thorn in our flesh. Speaking on backsliding,
Charles Spurgeon said to his congregation on March 13, 1870,
"I fear the disease is so rife among the people of God that there
is scarcely one of us who has not at some time or other suffered
from it."[5]

> If there is one consideration more humbling than another to a
> spiritually-minded believer, it is, that, after all God has done for
> him,—after all the rich displays of his grace, the patience and
> tenderness of his instructions, . . . the tokens of love received,
> and the lessons of experience learned, there should still exist in

---

4. Plumer, 148.

5. Charles Spurgeon, *The Metropolitan Tabernacle Pulpit: Sermons* (London:
Passmore & Alabaster, 1871), 145. The remainder of Spurgeon's sentence adds: "and
I fear that the most of us might confess if we judged our own hearts rightly, that in
some measure we are backsliding even now." I think I understand the sense of what
Spurgeon says here, especially considering his phrasing "in some measure." Yet my
definition of backsliding as something more obvious and sustained rather than our
general failures as Christians leads me to say that I likely wouldn't try to cast such
doubt on my own flock that they are all basically backsliders. If everyone is a backslider, then nobody is a backslider.

the heart a principle, the tendency of which is to secret, perpetual, and alarming departure from God.

So wrote Octavius Winslow, a nineteenth-century pastor and contemporary of Charles Spurgeon and of J. C. Ryle, in his outstanding work *Personal Declension and Revival of Religion in the Soul.*[6] Truly, few children of God are exempt from the humbling acknowledgment that we quickly and easily depart from living for God as we turn away from our Savior and thus grieve the Spirit.

Do you sense a general decline in faithful biblical zeal toward God in the church today? I do not think we can argue that things are worse now than they have ever been. This seems hard to prove and reveals a naive understanding about church history and people. Naturally, we tend to think that we are now living in a time of real spiritual distress. And in a sense, we are! If statistics are to be believed, as well as common observations, since roughly 2015 we have been facing a "de-churching crisis," so to speak.

We are living in precarious times. Yet the Puritan John Owen felt the same way in his day. In his work *On the Nature of Apostasy*, he opens "To the Reader" by arguing:

> That the state of religion is at this day deplorable in most parts of the Christian world is acknowledged by all who concern themselves in any thing that is so called. . . . The whole world is so evidently filled with the dreadful effects of the lusts of men, and sad tokens of divine displeasure, that all things from above and here below proclaim the degeneracy of our religion, in its profession, from its pristine beauty and glory.[7]

---

6. Octavius Winslow, *Personal Declension and Revival of Religion in the Soul* (Eugene, OR: Wipf and Stock, 2001), 9.

7. John Owen, *The Works of John Owen*, ed. W. H. Goold, 24 vols. (Edinburgh: T&T Clark, 1850–53), 7:3.

One wonders what Owen might have to say today (probably a lot!).

We should not think that we are the worst of all, but we also need to be careful not to think that we are experiencing an age of unprecedented blessing. Speaking as a pastor, I see the reality of the recent worldwide global pandemic (COVID-19) as exacerbating certain issues that were likely present in the church but are now openly manifest in unique ways (e.g., lack of or indifference to hospitality).

Many Christians are lamenting their own personal declension during the past few years. Some seem genuinely concerned about their continued personal apathy and lukewarmness toward the things of the Lord, but they are not quite sure how to "rebound" and rediscover their first love. Others appear to be aware that their Christian living does not look or feel as it used to, but they seem indifferent about their malaise. Many willfully miss corporate worship, and their consciences don't appear to prick them as they may have in the past because these people are living off various excuses that no longer seem entirely justifiable. Some still claim to watch online services, but even those who do so will admit that they tend to watch when convenient and often with little attention.

We can have some sympathy for how difficult many aspects of Christian living have become because of the pandemic. Christian fellowship and hospitality, for instance, were relegated to Zoom meetings in many countries, which simply catalyzed a struggle with being inhospitable toward others and so toward the Lord (Matt. 25:40). Even so, that does not change the reality for many that they are backsliding. Indeed, many parents are realizing how their children have not made great progress in the past few years, and so their concern is heightened by the stress they feel about the spiritual condition of their beloved offspring—and many of these parents will humbly acknowledge that they share some blame for the spiritual lethargy, indifference, and ignorance in their children.

Such manifestations of spiritual lethargy and unfaithfulness reveal a spirit of backsliding that must be repented of. Indeed, backsliding of any sort is extremely serious in God's eyes. In the words of Thomas Adams, "backsliding has ever been a sin most odious to God; yes, it is a pack or bundle of sins trussed up together, all derogatory to his honor, and contrary to his nature."[8] We reveal our hypocrisy to a God of truth; we reveal our inconstancy to a God who does not change; we reveal our infidelity to a faithful God; and we reveal our ingratitude to a gracious God.[9]

There must (and can) be a return to God and Christ by the Spirit. Hosea, concerned with Baal-worship in the northern kingdom that primarily manifested itself in sexual idolatry, pleads, "Return, O Israel, to the LORD your God, for you have stumbled because of your iniquity" (Hos. 14:1). Repentance leads to life and promises:

> I will heal their apostasy;
>> I will love them freely,
>>> for my anger has turned from them. (Hos. 14:4)

God's love is a drawing, wooing love to himself for the repentant backslider; it is a free love: "I will love them freely." But repentance is not a guarantee, as the Scriptures plainly testify. There are some who either slowly or quickly depart from the Lord and apparently never return. Peter and Judas jumped into a cauldron of sin, but only Peter emerged from it. As Andrew Fuller notes in his perceptive work *The Backslider*, "But whatever difference there be between a partial and a total departure from God, it will be difficult, if not impossible, for the party himself at the time to perceive it."[10] Similarly, Richard Bax-

---

8. Thomas Adams, *An Exposition upon the Second Epistle General of St. Peter* (London: Henry G. Bohn, 1848), 570.

9. Adams, 570.

10. Andrew Fuller, *The Backslider* (London: Hamilton, Adams, and Co., 1840), 19. Sinclair Ferguson likewise notes: "The solemn fact is that none of us can tell

ter wisely remarked that "partial backsliding has a natural tendency to total apostasy, and would effect it, if special grace did not prevent it."[11] The slippery slope does exist, and some who slide continue on it till they fall off into eternal darkness and despair.

We must reckon with the fact that the Scriptures offer plenty of salient examples of total abandonment from the faith. This is called *apostasy.* "After having made a profession of the true religion," says Fuller, "they apostatize from it." He adds: "I am aware it is common to consider a backslider as being a good man, though in a bad state of mind: but the scriptures do not confine the term to this application. . . . Backsliding, it is true, always supposes a profession of the true religion; but it does not necessarily suppose the existence of the thing professed. There is a perpetual backsliding, a drawing back unto perdition."[12] We cannot merely consider backsliding without therefore also considering the consequence of unrepentant backsliding: apostasy.

The goal of this book is not merely to establish the fact of backsliding and apostasy, but to diagnose it in such a way that we are aware of the dangers and symptoms of drifting from the Lord and so apply the various remedies offered by God in his Word for healing the backslidden soul. I am incapable of preventing the total apostasy whereby it is impossible to be restored again to repentance (see Heb. 6:4–6). I can only hope to assist in alarming and awakening the backslider to the real threats and dangers of personal declension that lead to apostasy. So while the diagnosis is crucial, the remedy is even more so—and it must be one that wins backsliders back to God from their turning away.

---

the difference between the beginning of backsliding and the beginning of apostasy. Both look the same." "Apostasy and How It Happens," March 14, 2023, https://www .ligonier.org/learn/articles/apostasy-and-how-it-happens.

11. Richard Baxter, *The Reformed Pastor* [. . .] (London: James Nisbet & Co., 1860), 125.

12. Fuller, *The Backslider,* 16–17.

If you are reading this book, you may be concerned about your own spiritual condition or the spiritual condition of others you love, and so you are seeking help. Or you are someone, perhaps even a pastor, who senses that something is not quite right with some of your people, and you are looking for help on how to recognize and deal with the dangers you are witnessing. May God be pleased to help all pastors develop such a caring sensitivity toward their wayward congregants. Or you may be a concerned family member who fears for the soul of a loved one. Many of us find ourselves in that position at some point in our lives. Take comfort; the Lord's arm is not too short to save (Isa. 59:1), and his arm is his Son, Jesus Christ, who finds his sheep and brings them back into the fold. But those who wander must be identified so that they may be found.

"I once was lost, but now am found," from the hymn "Amazing Grace!,"[13] could in fact have some application to the returning backslider, who, we pray, can again sing those words with a new-found fervor for God's patient, unchanging, amazing grace.

13. John Newton, "Amazing Grace!" (1779).

1

The Testimony of Scripture

O Backsliders, your case is a fearful one. (Thomas Boston)[1]

Backsliding and Apostasy

In the beginning, Adam and Eve fell away from God, which led to their departure from the temple of the Lord (Eden). While their case is unique compared to the rest of those in the church, given that they lived in both the prefall and postfall periods, they were first to turn away from God and, in a certain sense, play the role of backsliders and apostates. Excommunicated from the Edenic temple, they were gloriously recovered by God's promise (Gen. 3:15) and brought back into fellowship with him, albeit as those who would live with indwelling sin for the remainder of their lives on earth.

Since the time of the fall, the Bible, from Genesis to Revelation, reveals a disturbing catalogue of examples of backsliders and apostates from among the people of God. But the Bible also

---

1. Thomas Boston, *The Whole Works of Thomas Boston*, 12 vols. (Aberdeen: George and Robert King, 1852), 11:390.

1

reveals a patient, forgiving, gracious God so that backsliders do not need to remain on that path.

Backsliding is, as we would expect, a heart issue. So too is total apostasy, but in a different way. The latter reveals a heart of stone that has resisted the Holy Spirit in distinct ways. Apostates were at one time a type of backslider, but not all backsliders—praise God!—are necessarily apostates. A true Christian may backslide, but a saint who has been given the gift of supernatural faith from above cannot ultimately apostatize from the faith. Weak grace for those in Christ always proves victorious. An apostate who never returns to the Lord may have professed faith in Christ, but such a person was never truly engrafted into Christ to bear fruit in keeping with repentance, though he or she may have experienced many spiritual realities.

Archibald Alexander, in his excellent work *Thoughts on Religious Experience,* has a section on backsliding in which he not only distinguishes between perpetual and temporary backsliding, but also notes that those who live consistently godly lives can experience "short seasons of comparative coldness and insensibility" so that they "have not always equal light, and life, and comfort, in the divine life."[2] These are common occurrences in the lives of faithful Christians and should not necessarily be termed *backsliding.* Rather, backsliding is something whereby a Christian is "gradually led off from close walking with God, loses the lively sense of divine things, becomes too much attached to the world and too much occupied with secular concerns; until at length the keeping of the heart is neglected, closet duties are omitted or slightly performed, zeal for the advancement of religion is quenched, and many things once rejected by a sensitive conscience, are now indulged and defended."[3] In other words, much of Christian obedience gets thrown off course.

2. Archibald Alexander, *Thoughts on Religious Experience* (Philadelphia: Presbyterian Board of Publication, 1841), 206.

3. Alexander, 207.

In this book, we are concerned not so much with "short seasons" (e.g., a bad day or week) when we feel a little cold in our spiritual experience, but with formal backsliding and its relation to apostasy. Theologians who have addressed this matter have wisely stayed away from assigning definite periods of time to when spiritual sloth becomes formal backsliding. If we were to argue that three weeks of indifference to spiritual things constitutes backsliding, some might allow themselves two and a half weeks of "casual Christianity." I confess to not wishing to assign a definite period for that reason, but I think one should certainly be careful when days of ignoring God and Christ quickly turn to weeks and months. There can be no room for allowing ourselves a holiday from serving Christ. He calls us to daily denial (Luke 9:23). Total apostasy, however, can be more easily defined in terms of a definite period insofar as the true apostate does not ultimately return to the faith.

The Scottish theologian Ebenezer Erskine makes the distinction between "a total, as also a partial defection or falling off from Christ."[4] The wicked (reprobate) constitute the former (i.e., total), whereas the godly can fall into the latter (i.e., partial). Erskine adds that the godly may temporarily turn away from the Lord, "for they may be left for a considerable time, to make many woeful steps of defection from Christ and his ways." "But," he says, "when they fall, they are like wood or cork falling into water, who though they sink at first, yet they rise again by faith and repentance."[5] True believers may even fall in such a way as to be labeled apostate, but they will return to the fold because grace will prove victorious. As John Flavel remarks in his work *The Fountain of Life*: "though believers are not privileged from

4. Ebenezer Erskine, *The Whole Works of the Rev. Ebenezer Erskine: Consisting of Sermons and Discourses on Important and Interesting Subjects* [. . .], 3 vols. (London: William Baynes and Son, 1826), 1:24.

5. Erskine, 1:24.

backslidings, yet they are secured from final apostasy and ruin. The new creature may be sick, it cannot die. Saints may fall, but they shall rise again (Mic. 7:8)."[6]

Chapter 17 of the Westminster Confession of Faith, "Of the Perseverance of the Saints," acknowledges the fact of backsliding. While affirming the final perseverance of all true believers (17.1–2), the divines also recognized that some true believers may "through the temptations of Satan and of the world, the prevalence of corruption remaining in them, and the neglect of the means of their perseverance, fall into grievous sins; and for a time continue therein: whereby they incur God's displeasure, and grieve his Holy Spirit; come to be deprived of some measure of their graces and comforts; have their hearts hardened, and their consciences wounded; hurt and scandalise others, and bring temporal judgments upon themselves" (WCF 17.3).

In the following chapter in the confession (18.4), we are told that true Christians in their backsliding can experience an attack on their assurance of faith. As they are negligent in spiritual duties (e.g., prayer, public worship) and as they sometimes fall into a pattern of willful sinning for a period (e.g., habitual drunkenness, consistent use of pornography), their consciences are wounded, and they grieve the Holy Spirit. God can withdraw "the light of his countenance" and allow such people to, for a time, "walk in darkness and to have no light." As the divines made clear, however, "yet are they never utterly destitute of that seed of God, and life of faith, that love of Christ and the brethren, that sincerity of heart and conscience of duty, out of which, by the operation of the Spirit, this assurance may in due time be revived, and by the which, in the meantime, they are supported from utter despair" (WCF 18.4). This is an apt

---

6. John Flavel, *The Works of the Rev. Mr. John Flavel*, 6 vols. (1820; repr., Edinburgh: Banner of Truth, 1997), 1:352.

description of a backslider who has returned to communion with God.

The divines say things about the backslider that today we sometimes deny or feel embarrassed to affirm. The idea that believers can bring temporal judgments on themselves, receive God's displeasure, and walk in darkness without the light of God's countenance is practically denied by many preachers who, in some cases, would witness some strange and perhaps even angry looks if they ever spoke of these things from the pulpit with even an ounce of conviction.

Now, we need to be reminded that this is a book primarily for and about professing Christians or those who once made a profession of faith but seem to be walking in darkness away from the presence of the light of the Lord. *Backslider* refers to a person who is still part of the visible church and has not abandoned the faith altogether. *Apostate* does not describe every unbeliever in the world. Rather, an apostate once belonged to the visible church by way of profession. Apostates make "shipwreck of their faith" and are thus handed over to Satan (1 Tim. 1:19–20). They go out from the church, but they were not of the people of God, "for if they had been of us," says John, "they would have continued with us. But they went out, that it might become plain that they all are not of us" (1 John 2:19). Apostates incur greater guilt on themselves than pagans living in a land where the gospel has not reached them. Exposed and disgraced false teachers in the church are guiltiest of the worst forms of apostasy, as Peter explains: "For if, after they have escaped the defilements of the world through the knowledge of our Lord and Savior Jesus Christ, they are again entangled in them and overcome, the last state has become worse for them than the first" (2 Peter 2:20). Since teachers will be judged more strictly (James 3:1), apostate false teachers have a weighty judgment awaiting them.

Backsliding and apostasy are church-related issues, in one way or another. A group of unreached people may not believe in the

See also xviii

Son of God for forgiveness of their sins, but they are not those who are described in this book.

Old Testament Examples

Backsliding and apostasy frequently happened in the Old Testament. It happened to individuals (e.g., Esau, Lot's wife). King Asa is one example among many. While the Chronicler has a generally favorable view of his reign, in the last five years of his life Asa backslides and fails to trust in God as he should, preferring instead to trust in alliances with foreigners (2 Chron. 16:1–14). Asa appears to even receive punishment for his sin (v. 12). Not just individuals, but corporately we see backsliding and apostasy among God's people (see Numbers; Judges).

Deuteronomy describes "certain worthless fellows," who left the people of God to serve other gods (Deut. 13:13). In Jeremiah's time, Judah forsook the Lord and instead trusted in pagan allies such as Egypt and Assyria, whose gods could not protect them (Jer. 1:16). Thus, Jeremiah declares:

> Your evil will chastise you,
>   and your apostasy will reprove you.
> Know and see that it is evil and bitter
>   for you to forsake the Lord your God;
>   the fear of me is not in you,
> declares the Lord God of hosts. (Jer. 2:19)

What is called "apostasy" is later called "perpetual backsliding" in Jeremiah 8:5:

> Why then has this people turned away
>   in perpetual backsliding?
> They hold fast to deceit;
>   they refuse to return.

Same Hebrew?

Both amount to a turning away from the Lord, a forsaking of faithful covenant relations. And while for the purposes of this book we are distinguishing the two, the Scriptures tend to see them in very close relation, and so must we.

The book of Judges is another clear example of Israel's backsliding and apostasy. In Judges 2:11–15, God's people served the Baals and thus abandoned the Lord—they abandoned their God who had rescued them from Egypt. Going after other gods, they provoked the Lord, who handed them over to their enemies. Despite their terrible distress, they did not listen. We know this because a constant refrain emerges in the book of Judges, "And the people of Israel did what was evil in the sight of the LORD" (2:11; 3:7; 4:1; 6:1; 10:6; 13:1). Various kings, as well, did what was evil in the sight of the Lord (e.g., 1 Kings 15:26, 34; 2 Kings 21:20).

Many more examples could be offered. Whether recorded in the Major Prophets (e.g., Isaiah, Jeremiah) or the Minor Prophets (e.g., Hosea, Amos), God's people in the Old Testament were constantly turning away from the Lord, and in many cases the judgments they received were testimonies to the seriousness of their offenses. For to whom much is given, much is expected (Luke 12:48).

New Testament Examples

In the New Testament, the reality of backsliding and apostasy does not simply disappear because of the stability and glories of the new covenant. Sadly, the dangers are littered all over the pages of the New Testament, with even whole books (e.g., Hebrews, Revelation) given to warning Christians about the dangers of falling away and the need to remain faithful to Christ as the only hope for salvation in a world that will one day be judged.

The author of Hebrews seems to make both backsliding and apostasy a central focus of the letter—not just in the obvious

3:12-15

places (Heb. 6:4–6; 10:25–29), but throughout the letter from beginning to end. In fact, in the letter, Old Testament examples (e.g., Ps. 95) serve as a warning for Christians living in the new covenant (Heb. 3–4). For one thing, the author seems to be concerned that all his hearers take seriously the dangers of "an evil, unbelieving heart," which can lead people "to fall away from the living God" (3:12). The deceitfulness of sin can harden us and lead to rebellion against God (vv. 13–15).

Our Lord confronts the seven churches, sometimes with startling warnings. To the church in Ephesus he says: "Remember therefore from where you have fallen; repent, and do the works you did at first. If not, I will come to you and remove your lampstand from its place, unless you repent" (Rev. 2:5). And in the letter to the church in Laodicea, the backsliding Laodiceans are warned that their pride and complacency may lead to a judgment of apostasy. Jesus declares: "I know your works: you are neither cold nor hot. Would that you were either cold or hot! So, because you are lukewarm, and neither hot nor cold, I will spit you out of my mouth. For you say, I am rich, I have prospered, and I need nothing, not realizing that you are wretched, pitiable, poor, blind, and naked" (3:15–17). The Lord, who stands rejected outside the church, in his grace yet knocks and offers restoration if they repent. But Jesus warns them because he loves them ("Those whom I love, I reprove and discipline, so be zealous and repent," v. 19). This type of pastoral care from Christ cannot be questioned, though one might quietly think that Jesus may be speaking a little too harshly for our modern sensibilities. The reality of his words shows us that sometimes entire congregations can spiritually drift.

None of the examples offered should surprise us if we have given even a passing reading to the Gospels. In the parable of the sower, Jesus highlights various types of people. There is a certain type of hearer ("sown on rocky ground," Matt. 13:20) who hears the Word and even receives it with joy. Such a person "has no root in himself, but endures for a while, and when tribulation or persecution arises on account of the word, immediately he falls away" (v. 21). This is a falling away, an apostasy.

Turning from the Lord is serious. Lot's wife "looked back" and was destroyed (Gen. 19:26; see also Luke 9:62, "No one who puts his hand to the plow and looks back is fit for the kingdom of God"). Jesus dealt with disciples who "turned back and no longer walked with him" (John 6:66). God does not delight in "those who shrink back and are destroyed" (Heb. 10:38–39). Christian living is a going forward, but backsliding is just that: a going backward. And sometimes that "backward" eventually manifests itself, if there is no repentance, in apostasy. It is a running from God to another god and becoming like that god (Pss. 115:4–8; 135:15–18).

Many people in the church are fond of the saying, "Major on the majors, minor on the minors." Naturally, there is some truth in this, if only we can all agree on what the "majors" and "minors" are! But if we are going to adopt such an approach to pastoral ministry, it may mean a great many more warnings about the dangers of backsliding and apostasy than we are comfortable with. Our Lord did not hesitate to warn his hearers, and neither did the author of Hebrews.

Besides the Westminster Confession, the Canons of Dort explain how the warnings have a positive use in the perseverance of the saints. In an English translation from the authorized Latin version in the Fifth Head of Doctrine ("Of the Perseverance of the Saints"), article 14, we read: "As it has pleased God to begin his work of grace in us by the preaching of the gospel, so he preserves, continues and perfects it through the hearing, reading, meditation, exhortations, threatenings, [and] promises of that same gospel, and also through the use of the sacraments."[7] God

---

7. John Owen writes in connection with a gospel threat: "A fond conceit has befallen some, that all denunciations of future wrath, even unto believers, is legal, which therefore it does not become the preachers of the gospel to insist upon: *so*

preserves his people through many means, including promises and threats.

Indeed, the apostle Paul, writing to the Corinthians, has a rather long and important section on just this point. After reminding his hearers of the wickedness of certain Old Testament saints, with whom God was not pleased, and the subsequent judgments from God, Paul tells the Corinthians that these past historical events among God's people "took place as examples for us, that we might not desire evil as they did" (1 Cor. 10:6). We should avoid the various temptations to turn away from the Lord to idolatry. These past acts of infidelity by those who claimed to be God's people should instruct us (v. 11) and cause us not to be overconfident. After all, warns Paul, "let anyone who thinks that he stands take heed lest he fall" (v. 12).

The facts of biblical history tell us that all too often God's people did not find the infinite God satisfactory, lovely, and sufficient. God's goodness was deemed unacceptable, unenticing, and uninteresting. And when this happened, it was a type of practical atheism. The apostate is denying the God that he or she once claimed to know through Christ, and this, according to Stephen Charnock, "is a greater affront to deny him, after an experience of his sweetness and assistance, than to deny him before any dealing with him, or trial of him."[8] He adds that "though all apostasy begins in a neglect, yet it quickly ripens into a hatred."[9] The apostate hates

---

would men make themselves wiser than Jesus Christ and all his apostles, yes, they would disarm the Lord Christ, and expose him to the contempt of his vilest enemies. There is also, we see, a great use in these *evangelical threatenings* to believers themselves. And they have been observed to have had an effectual ministry, both unto conversion and edification, who have been made wise and dexterous in managing gospel [threats] toward the consciences of their hearers. And those that hear the word may hence learn their duty, when such threatenings are handled and opened to them." *The Works of John Owen*, ed. W. H. Goold, 24 vols. (Edinburgh: T&T Clark, 1850–53), 3:287.

8. Stephen Charnock, *The Complete Works of Stephen Charnock*, 5 vols. (Edinburgh: James Nichol, 1864–66; repr., Edinburgh: Banner of Truth, 1985), 5:492.

9. Charnock, 5:492.

God. The backslider needs to be warned that drifting from God is a secret type of hatred that, sadly, left unchecked can become open hatred.

Application

What lessons can we glean from this brief look at examples from God's Word?

First, God warns his people of their turning away from him in order that they may turn back to him through faith and repentance. This is a note that will sound often in this book because it is a note that is often sounded in God's Word. Pastoral care requires warnings when there is a need to be warned! One should not go around frightening the godly, who, while conscious of their sin, are living in fellowship with God and his people. But we do have a duty to those who have become lukewarm. Christ makes promises to backsliders in Ephesus and Laodicea (see Rev. 2:7; 3:20–21). True, his threats are real, but so too are his offers of mercy and grace. If a doctor told a sick patient that all was well, we would accuse such a physician of malpractice. Sadly, many pastors today are too afraid to confront backsliders, and this may reveal a backslidden pastor. But the pastor also needs to hold out the same promises and comforts to backsliders (who repent) that we see in God's Word. If we are so sure that there is a remedy for a disease, we should not shy away from exposing a spiritual illness.

Second, the discussion above has shown that turning away from the Lord is a predominant theme in the biblical story. We can, however, distinguish between a total falling away (apostasy) and a temporary turning away (backsliding). It is hard to distinguish the two when the person is in the process of turning away from the Lord. But John Owen makes an important point that "it may be given as a safe rule in general, that he who is spiritually sensible of the evil of his backsliding is unquestionably in a recoverable condition; and some may be so who are not yet sensible thereof, so long as they are capable of being made so by convictions. No man is past hopes of salvation until he is past all possibility of repentance; and no man is past all possibility of repentance until he be absolutely hardened against all gospel convictions."[10] There is always hope unless a person is "absolutely hardened" against the gospel. And when one is sensible of his or her own lukewarmness, then we have hope that gospel light will begin to shine on the darkness that has—we pray—only temporarily entered the soul.

For Further Reflection

1. Can you think of some other examples of backsliding and apostasy in the Scriptures that were not mentioned in this chapter?
2. What is the difference between backsliding and apostasy?
3. Do you see this danger in the church today? If so, how?
4. Read and meditate on Hosea 14; 1 Corinthians 10:1–12; Hebrews 3–4.

The Bible repeatedly warns us of backsliding and apostasy in both OT and NT

10. Owen, *Works*, 7:236.

2

The Pilgrim's Progress

For grace is given, not because we have done good works, but in order that we may be able to do them: that is, not because we have fulfilled the Law, but in order that we may be able to fulfil it. (Augustine)[1]

Awkward Running

Imagine a young lady who has been paralyzed from a horrible fall suffered during a trail race. Surgeons tell her that she will never walk again, never mind run. A medical miracle occurs, allowing movement back in her legs and then, amazingly, the ability to slowly walk with help but without fluidity of movement. Ongoing therapy leads to better walking and a new goal of one day being able to run again. She rightly keeps moving, rehabilitating, exercising, and so on, but days and weeks of mental and physical roadblocks partly undo the good work of the previous few months. Despite several such setbacks, in a few years she finally jogs one mile. She experiences more complications, but after many years finally runs a ten-kilometer race. Her goal is simply to finish, but

1. Augustine, *On the Spirit and the Letter*, trans. W. J. Sparrow-Simpson (London: Society for Promoting Christian Knowledge, 1925), 53.

it is a glorious victory, even with her somewhat awkward stride. Most onlookers have no idea of the history behind this momentous occasion or what the celebration is all about. Yet this race of approximately ten thousand steps has come after total inactivity, involving not only a miracle but also many ups and downs, loads of help and encouragement, countless steps backward, and lots of tears—both of joy and of sorrow. But in the end, she runs the race set before her, even though with great difficulty.

The Christian life parallels the scenario above. As we make progress, our "movement" will always be awkward because of indwelling sin. However clumsily, we still move forward, making progress toward the finish as we run the race set before us (2 Tim. 4:7–8; Heb. 12:1–3). Backsliders in the church sinfully run in the wrong direction, yet can get moving forward on the right path again by God's grace.

Before looking at the causes and cures of backsliding, we must consider the Scriptures' teaching on God's children making forward progress: "But grow in the grace and knowledge of our Lord and Savior Jesus Christ" (2 Peter 3:18). Living as justified saints and with many promises of Christ (2 Cor. 1:20), we must, charges the apostle Paul, "cleanse ourselves from every defilement of body and spirit, bringing holiness to completion in the fear of God" (7:1). "A good Christian," argues Thomas Watson, "is not like Hezekiah's Sun that went backward, nor Joshua's Sun that stood still, but is always advancing in Holiness, and increasing with the Increase of God" (see Col. 2:19).[2]

Related to this forward movement, we ask the same questions at the heart of many books on Christian living and sanctification: (1) How do we grow in grace as Christians? (2) What does this growth look like? (3) What is the end goal of our growth?

---

2. Thomas Watson, *A Body of Practical Divinity* [...] (London: Thomas Parkhurst, 1692), 215.

The Work of Sanctification

Those united to Christ by faith receive the benefits of his salvation, not only the grace of forgiveness and acceptance in our Savior as children of God, but also the grace of transformation in the image of God's Son. This latter change, namely, sanctification, occurs both immediately (definitively) and over time (progressively) as we are new creations in Christ (1 Cor. 1:2; 2 Cor. 5:17). Sanctification consists of two parts, generally speaking: mortification and vivification. The former relates to the "killing" of sin (Rom. 8:13); the latter relates to our growth in holiness (Eph. 4:24). The answer to question 35 of the Westminster Shorter Catechism sums up this two-pronged grace quite well: "Sanctification is the work of God's free grace, whereby we are renewed in the whole man after the image of God, and are enabled more and more to die unto sin, and live unto righteousness." Sin is not only a positive inclination toward evil, but also a privation (a lack) of what is good and righteous. Christ provides the answer to these two problems.

Thomas Goodwin calls us "empty creatures" by nature.[3] Jesus intervened to give abundant life (John 10:10) to such dead creatures, a life of grace, "the main properties" of which, maintains Goodwin, "are to move and grow. . . . [Grace] is an active thing, and it is a growing thing also; and because the more it is acted the more it grows, therefore its growth is expressed by its motion."[4] Christians must hold fast to Christ because he gives nourishment and development, "with a growth that is from God" (Col. 2:19).

The Holy Spirit enables us in Christ to turn from a life in the flesh to a new one in the Spirit (Rom. 8:1–10) as we put off the old self and put on the new self, which is "created after the likeness of God in true righteousness and holiness" (Eph. 4:22–24). Paul

---

3. Thomas Goodwin, *The Works of Thomas Goodwin*, 12 vols. (Edinburgh: James Nichol, 1861–66; repr., Grand Rapids: Reformation Heritage Books, 2006), 3:457.
4. Goodwin, 3:457.

exhorts justified Christians, who are now beyond condemnation (Rom. 8:1), to "put to death the deeds of the body" by the power of the Holy Spirit (v. 13). The Spirit keeps us from a "fall back into fear" (v. 15) as we live life freely as God's adopted children while patiently awaiting our future glorification (v. 17).

As we will see, Christian growth does not happen automatically, though it occurs as the desired outcome based on the promises of God. We must not think that the virtues of faith, hope, and love are omnipotent or that they simply "work" because their origin is from above. Octavius Winslow rightly observes that we can wrongly deify these virtues, "forgetting that though they undoubtedly are divine in their origin, spiritual in their nature, and sanctifying in their effects, they yet are sustained by no self-supporting power, but by constant communications of life and nourishment from Jesus; that, the moment of their being left to their inherent strength, is the moment of their certain declension and decay."[5] Sanctification necessarily brings progress, but graces need to be fed. Faith, for example, must feed on Christ (John 6:35, 51), who gives himself in his Word and sacraments. Believers, failing to spiritually eat and drink, should not be surprised when spiritual emaciation takes place. Sanctification is a work of God's grace, yet involves believers, who work out their salvation with fear and trembling while God works in them (Phil. 2:12–13). Those who "work out" are those in whom God works.

Growth in grace does not occur with the simple idea to "Let go, and let God," for such an approach makes us entirely passive with no active role in dying to sin and living to righteousness. Indeed, we are entirely dependent on Christ for this work in us. As Jonathan Edwards rightly notes, sanctification is totally our work, but only because it is totally God's work: "In efficacious grace we

---

5. Octavius Winslow, *Personal Declension and Revival of Religion in the Soul* (Eugene, OR: Wipf and Stock, 2001), 10.

are not merely passive, nor yet does God do some and we do the rest. But God does all, and we do all. God produces all, we act all. For that is what he produces, viz. [namely] our own acts. God is the only proper author and fountain; we only are the proper actors. We are in different respects, wholly passive and wholly active."[6]

Christ's Progress

God sustains us through Christ, just as the Father nourished him on earth as he "increased in wisdom and in stature and in favor with God and man" (Luke 2:52). The pattern of Christian growth is Christ, who grew up in wisdom and maturity as a faithful Son, and a Prophet, Priest, and King for his people. How did this happen? Jesus lived by faith, trusting every word that came from the mouth of God (Matt. 4:4). In the third Servant Song, we read of the life of the Servant, Jesus Christ himself:

> The Lord GOD has given me
>   the tongue of those who are taught,
> that I may know how to sustain with a word
>   him who is weary.
> Morning by morning he awakens;
>   he awakens my ear
>   to hear as those who are taught.
> The Lord GOD has opened my ear,
>   and I was not rebellious;
>   I turned not backward. (Isa. 50:4–5)

Our Lord clearly testified that his teaching was not his own, but the Father's (John 7:16). Indeed, he spoke only the words

---

6. Jonathan Edwards, *The Works of President Edwards*, 4 vols. (New York: Leavitt & Allen, 1856), 2:580.

that the Father had given him (12:49). Still, he had to learn what to say and how to speak. The Servant Song above affirms this morning-by-morning instruction. How this exactly happened remains unclear, but we can be certain that he continually and habitually devoured the Old Testament Scriptures over the course of his lifetime. He would have memorized and perfectly interpreted the Old Testament.

When kings came into office, they were to copy down the law (Deut. 17:18). Jesus, no doubt, internalized this law in his mind and heart. Indeed, most frequently during his public ministry he asked this question: "Have you not read . . . ?" (e.g., Matt. 12:3). He asked not Gentiles without much knowledge of the Old Testament Scriptures, but deeply religious Jews.

For the thirty years before his public ministry, Jesus grew in learning, yet foundationally taught from above (Ps. 22:9–10). Then for roughly three years, he taught others with his Father's words. He possessed a "tongue of those who are taught" and an ear "to hear as those who are taught" (Isa. 50:4) to sustain the weary. He alone is suited to give progress in the Christian life and bring back the backslider.

Isaiah 50:5–6 further expresses our Lord's willing and obedient service:

> The Lord God has opened my ear,
>   and I was not rebellious;
>   I turned not backward.
> I gave my back to those who strike,
>   and my cheeks to those who pull out the beard;
> I hid not my face
>   from disgrace and spitting.

Everything Christ did for us and our salvation he accomplished willingly. Here he claims repeatedly, "I—I—I did it," as he does in the New Testament: "I lay down my life for the sheep" (John 10:15); "No one takes [my life] from me" (v. 18). All through the Bible, Christ testifies in essence: "I gave them my body to nail on the cross. I did it because I was willing."

Learning obedience through his various trials and sufferings occurred in the power of the Spirit. Without him, there can be no spiritual life or progress in godliness and maturity. The Old Testament clearly stresses the Spirit's role in resting on the Messiah, as in these passages from the prophet Isaiah:

> And the Spirit of the LORD shall rest upon him,
>> the Spirit of wisdom and understanding,
>> the Spirit of counsel and might,
>> the Spirit of knowledge and the fear of the LORD.
> (Isa. 11:2)

> Behold my servant, whom I uphold,
>> my chosen, in whom my soul delights;
> I have put my Spirit upon him;
>> he will bring forth justice to the nations. (Isa. 42:1)

> The Spirit of the Lord GOD is upon me,
>> because the LORD has anointed me
> to bring good news to the poor;
>> he has sent me to bind up the brokenhearted,
> to proclaim liberty to the captives,
>> and the opening of the prison to those who are bound.
> (Isa. 61:1)

Indeed, Jesus' own growth in obedience through the power of the Spirit establishes the fact of our own obedience. "Although he was a son," we read, "he learned obedience through what he suffered" (Heb. 5:8). Our growth comes in like manner. In our union with Christ, we enter his life and share in his glories, but also in his life of suffering. We have the mind of Christ (1 Cor. 2:16) because we possess the Spirit of Christ (Rom. 8:9; 1 Peter 1:11).

Our predestination leads to our growth and progress in conformity to the image of Christ by the Spirit (Rom. 8:29) and so brings about our maturity. Paul hoped for the Ephesians that "all attain to the unity of the faith and of the knowledge of the Son of God, to mature manhood, to the measure of the stature of the fullness of Christ" (Eph. 4:13). All believers are to "grow up in every way into him who is the head, into Christ, from whom the whole body, joined and held together by every joint with which it is equipped, when each part is working properly, makes the body grow so that it builds itself up in love" (vv. 15–16). Christian growth is Christ-focused, and all united to him by faith are joined to the one who himself grew in obedience and trust toward God. Christ brought forth fruit and lived for God through the Spirit's aid graciously provided by his Father.

These, then, are the essential components of Christian living: from God, to God, and all through Christ by the Spirit.

Application

The opposite of backsliding is growing conformity to Christ. Our hope is in the promise of God, who unveils our faces to show us the glory of Christ and so transform us into his image, "from one degree of glory to another" (2 Cor. 3:18). If we take our eyes off Christ, we not only stagnate in the Christian life, but regress. As we move further into this book, we will see how we take our eyes off but can fix them back on Christ.

Still, we want to hold out hope here, as well, at the beginning of the book. Note well that Christ's victory through obedience to God and in the power of the Spirit establishes our own victory in the same way. So we rejoice that we, in faith and in faithful obedience, share in Christ's sufferings and will be glorified with him (1 Peter 4:13; 1 John 3:2). Indeed, when he returns, he "will transform our lowly body to be like his glorious body" (Phil. 3:21). Is this not what you ultimately want? To be fully conformed to Christ and one day look on him face to face on that glorious day? Until then, we must strive by faith for this conformity in this life as we are changed in Christ from one degree of glory to another. This is our hope, comfort, and joy in a world where we need every promise to keep us on that narrow path to life.

Paul connects conformity to Christ with the certainty of glorification: "For those whom he foreknew he also predestined to be conformed to the image of his Son, in order that he might be the firstborn among many brothers. And those whom he predestined he also called, and those whom he called he also justified, and those whom he justified he also glorified" (Rom. 8:29–30). Do not miss the incredible affirmation by Paul that Jesus is "the firstborn" among his brothers, as he progressed to glorification himself through his life and sufferings. Here, then, is the reason why we will as well, for those he justifies he certainly glorifies.

As Christ progressed in this world, you will too. As "strangers and pilgrims on the earth," we will make progress toward eternal glory and away from the "fleshly lusts" of this world (Heb. 11:13 KJV; 1 Peter 2:11 KJV). As the chapter title suggests, the pilgrims do indeed progress. Similarly, John Bunyan's allegory *The Pilgrim's Progress* (1678) affirms this as Christian escapes from the City of Destruction to the Celestial City. Along the way, he encounters a man locked in an iron cage because he had given himself over to the "Lusts, Pleasures, and Profits of this World" to a point of no return. He was a backslider who had so hardened his heart against Christ that he testified, "I *cannot* repent" (see Heb. 6:4–6;

10:26–29). So as we will see more fully, it is possible to drift away so far as a professing yet not true believer that there is no hope, as the man admits: "No, none at all." With this in mind, may we for now take up the resolve of Christian "to watch and be sober; and to pray, that I may shun the causes of this man's misery."[7]

Finally, please know that Christ is zealous for your progress. In Christ's cleansing of the temple, we find the words of Psalm 69:9 clearly referring to him: "Zeal for your house will consume me" (John 2:17). We should not doubt that his zeal for God's house remains, namely, for us as the church, the temple of the Lord: "Do you not know that you are God's temple and that God's Spirit dwells in you? If anyone destroys God's temple, God will destroy him. For God's temple is holy, and you are that temple" (1 Cor. 3:16–17; see also Eph. 2:19–22). Christ is consumed with zeal that his church be a holy temple becoming like him and through him, that he might "redeem us from all lawlessness and . . . purify for himself a people for his own possession who are zealous for good works" (Titus 2:14).

Yet this work occurs not in a vacuum without our own zeal. We must take an active role in making progress, in growing in conformity to Christ. Protection from a backsliding heart begins, then, with a resolve to be like Christ through Christ. Such resolve will wax and wane and need constant renewal. Like Christ, to grow you must feed daily on his Word, the very Scriptures on which he himself fed and so nurtured his consuming zeal. May the same be true of us. Rather than the things of this world easily and sinfully consuming us as backsliders, may we grow more and more in the zeal of the Lord, which cannot consume us enough, to the glory of God.

---

7. John Bunyan, *The Pilgrim's Progress*, ed. J. B. Wharey and Roger Sharrock (Oxford: Clarendon Press, 1960), 34–35.

(see p 17)

His own progress
↗ *—Word*
—Spirit

For Further Reflection

1. How does Christ's life affect our view of Christian progress?
2. Why is it important that Christians progress in this life?
3. What are some of the means God uses to make us like Christ?
4. Read and meditate on Isaiah 42:1–9; Romans 8:1–30; 2 Corinthians 3:12–4:6.

⟶ *We were made (and saved) to be like Christ*

⟶ *Word*
Spirit
Communion
Fellowship
Trials / Suffering
Eyes on Christ
Prayer

Our progress through life should be patterned after and toward Christ-likeness. By God's grace, we strike for it.

3

The Varieties of Christians

*It is a sad thing to be Christians at a supper, heathens in our shops,
and devils in our closets.* (Stephen Charnock)[1]

Visible-Invisible Church

Addressing the matter of backsliding in relation to God's
promises does not pose quite the same problems to our understanding of the Christian life as the problem of apostasy in relation
to the gracious nature of salvation. On the one hand, Christians
receive many assurances of salvation, including the dearly beloved
truths that "he who began a good work in you will bring it to
completion at the day of Jesus Christ" (Phil. 1:6) and that "those
whom he predestined he also called, and those whom he called
he also justified, and those whom he justified he also glorified"
(Rom. 8:30). On the other hand, however, while there is a promise
of entering God's rest for the faithful, we should fear, "lest any of
you should seem to have failed to reach it" (Heb. 4:1).

1. Stephen Charnock, *The Complete Works of Stephen Charnock*, 5 vols. (Edinburgh:
James Nichol, 1864–66; repr., Edinburgh: Banner of Truth, 1985), 4:400.

Tension between perseverance of saints and warnings

Christians receive promises of the power of God in saving sinners, but they also receive warnings to not fall away from the faith. How can we make sense of this by doing justice to the totality of biblical teaching on these matters? How do we affirm the unconditional aspects of salvation with the apparently conditional "ifs" that we find in God's Word (see Rom. 8:13; Col. 1:23)? Before answering these delicate questions, we must establish certain truths concerning the nature of the church.

Historically, many theologians have spoken about the visible and invisible church. This is a basic way of affirming that not all who publicly profess to be Christians are necessarily united to Christ by a saving faith that leads to glory. Thus, there are, as it were, unregenerate people in the church who are distinguished from regenerate people in the church, and only God knows precisely who is and is not elect.

Christ seems to teach this reality in Matthew 13:47–50, where he likens the kingdom of heaven to a net gathering fish of every kind and then separating the good from the bad at the end of the age. His parable of the sower (Matt. 13:1–9, 18–23) likewise reveals the "mixed" nature of the kingdom.

John Calvin observed that the Scriptures speak of the church in two ways: "Sometimes by the term 'church' it means that which is actually in God's presence, into which no persons are received but those who are children of God by grace of adoption and true members of Christ by sanctification of the Holy Spirit. . . . Often, however, the name 'church' designates the whole multitude of men spread over the earth who profess to worship one God and Christ. . . . In this church are mingled many hypocrites who have nothing of Christ but the name and outward appearance."[2] Calvin explains here what has popularly been described as the *visible-invisible church distinction*.

---

2. John Calvin, *Institutes of the Christian Religion*, ed. John T. McNeill, trans. Ford Lewis Battles, 2 vols. (Philadelphia: Westminster Press, 1960), 4.1.7.

Heidlberg
Catechism
↓

Zacharias Ursinus makes it clear, however, that the church is called *invisible*, "not that the men who are in it are invisible, but because the faith and piety of those who belong to it can neither be seen, nor known, except by those who possess it; and also because we cannot with certainty distinguish the godly from those who are hypocrites in the visible church."[3] Because we are finite, lacking comprehensive knowledge, we must accept that our abilities to discern between real and false believers is limited. So when we refer to someone as a "believer," we can speak of that person in terms of his or her outward profession. At the same time, we can acknowledge that calling someone a "believer" does not guarantee the reality of saving faith.

God alone knows infallibly who is truly united to his Son by the Spirit and who is not. We do not have such knowledge of the elect. Thus, the church, often through the elders who interview candidates for membership, makes judgments about the credibility of one's confession. The judgments that the church offers concerning those who profess to trust in Christ alone for salvation are termed *judgments of charity*. We cannot absolutely know what is in each person's heart, but according to a charitable judgment, we believe a credible confession of faith, and that person is thus treated as a Christian. As we know, often by painful experience, some abandon the church and their profession of Christ. What can we say about them? That they never had any spiritual blessings at all? Of course not, for we see in both the Old and New Testaments evidence of certain spiritual though nonsaving benefits to the unregenerate within the context of God's covenant community. Here is where we need to be exceedingly careful to do justice to what the Scriptures say.

3. Zacharias Ursinus, *Commentary on the Heidelberg Catechism* (Grand Rapids: Eerdmans, 1956), 287.

Types of Unions

In his work *The Trial of a Christian's Growth,* Thomas Goodwin offers some stimulating comments on John 15:1–2 and other passages regarding the differences between temporary and true believers. He asks the reader to "consider, that union with Christ is it that makes men branches; that is, men are accounted branches of Christ in regard of some union with him: and such as their union is, such also is their communion with him, and accordingly such branches are they, and such their fruit."[4]

Christ distinguishes between branches in him that do and do not bear fruit (John 15:2). There is in both cases talk of being "in him" as those united to the life-giving vine. This seems surprising, given that so many references in the New Testament to being "in Christ" are to the certainty of salvation.

Yet there are some who are united to Christ by "the external tie of the outward ordinances."[5] Such professing Christians possess a relationship with Christ that is merely external, as they partake of outward ordinances. They are "in him" in a highly qualified sense. This could refer to people who have been baptized, whether as children or adults, but who keep the church and Christ at a distance, even though they will often call themselves "Christians" because they were baptized. They may even attend church occasionally, at least on Christmas and Easter. There is no "sap or inward influence derived," that is, no inner working of the Spirit "or stirring of affection."[6] Their "fruit" is no different from that of unbelievers, such as telling the truth—albeit imperfectly and not from a regard for God's glory—that is a remnant of the image of God and common grace. They live a natural life rather than a

---

4. Thomas Goodwin, *The Works of Thomas Goodwin,* 12 vols. (Edinburgh: James Nichol, 1861–66; repr., Grand Rapids: Reformation Heritage Books, 2006), 3:440.

5. Goodwin, 3:440.

6. Goodwin, 3:441.

supernatural life in the sense that they operate from their own worldly strength and common gifts rather than those from above from Christ himself.

harder to tell types

But there is another type of professing Christian, according to Goodwin, who is also not necessarily elect. And this may be surprising to those who typically contrast the type of person above (i.e., the one who merely received an outward ordinance) with a true Christian. This other type of professing Christian in the church has received from Christ "some sap of his Spirit into their hearts, quickening them with many good motions, and stirring up some juiciness of affections in the administration of the word and sacraments, which causes them to bud forth into good inward purposes and outward good beginnings."[7] As Goodwin notes, however, this is not a communication of the Spirit "as sanctifying and changing the branch into the same nature with the root."[8] Such people "share" in the common work of the Spirit among God's worshiping community. *(non-salvific/regenerate)*

Heb 6:4

We are told by Christ that the seed sown on rocky ground is received by the person who receives the Word with joy (Matt. 13:20). But there is no root, and while this person endures in the church for a time, he or she eventually falls away because of various trials (v. 21). There is, as we read in Matthew 13, another type of ground that the seed falls on: the thorny ground—though the cares of the world keep the Word from having any real effect (v. 22). We should be careful about drawing too many fine distinctions *yeah* between these believers, especially in relation to the Spirit's work. But it may be profitable to acknowledge that some come closer than others to true salvation.

... No partial possession of Spirit + extra favor
No rejecting regeneration + the extra
Experience of participation in church blessings, work

Goodwin states of those who receive the Spirit but, while close, do not receive full salvation that "inward sap is communicated to

7. Goodwin, 3:441.
8. Goodwin, 3:441.

Maybe a positive but unregenerate experience within the New Cov community but without faith in Christ

them"; indeed, the Spirit is "communicated in a further degree, abides in them longer, shoots up farther, and these prove exceeding green branches, and are owned for true, even by the people of God themselves, as Judas was by the apostles, and therefore are outwardly like unto them."[9] Unlike those who have merely outward morals, as a result of natural law, these types of "believers" have, according to Goodwin, "a sap that puts a greenness into what they do, and by reason of which they bear and bring forth.... And these also have some kind of union with Christ as with a *Lord*, 2 Peter 2:1, ... so far to enable them to do him some service in his vineyard."[10] True, they are not united to Christ as a Head like true believers, and neither do they possess the Spirit of adoption. But these types, like Judas, receive some operations of the Spirit that enable them to do certain works of ministry (e.g., preaching, praying). They can have many gifts, despite lacking true lasting fruit (Gal. 5:22–23).

In his well-known work on apostasy, John Owen dissects Hebrews 6:4–6 in a manner that helps us understand the various types of believers that may exist in the visible church. The text speaks of those who have been "enlightened" to the point that they "have shared in the Holy Spirit" (Heb. 6:4). This illumination gives these types of believers some "delight and joy"[11] in the truths of the gospel, even to the point that the illumination received has some efficacy. Such people abstain from sin and perform many duties; they appear to be blameless in their conduct in this world and do not for a time bring any public reproach on Christ. Even so, this illumination has its limits.

Many temporary believers have been greatly affected by a sermon and have even offered prayers in private and in public. Some have even been ordained as elders or deacons. They "have

9. Goodwin, 3:441.

10. Goodwin, 3:441.

11. John Owen, *The Works of John Owen*, ed. W. H. Goold, 24 vols. (Edinburgh: T&T Clark, 1850–53), 21:76.

spiritual experience and knowledge but not spiritual rebirth (cf Judas)

tasted the heavenly gift, and have shared in the Holy Spirit, and have tasted the goodness of the word of God and the powers of the age to come" (Heb. 6:4–5). The metaphor used of "tasted" shows that there was, to some extent, an experience (personal involvement) of what was being offered. It may even have been pleasant at first. But there was, in the end, a refusal to digest what was offered and grow from the nutrients of the promises.

Our Lord speaks of those who said, "Lord, Lord," but failed to enter the kingdom because they did not do the will of God, but engaged in works that were lawless (Matt. 7:21–23). Interestingly, in a subtle proof of the perseverance of the true saints, Jesus says to these people that he casts away: "I never knew you" (v. 23). If these professors of the Lord had at one time been true Christians but had fallen away, he could not say to them that he never knew them.

With this said, we should be able to affirm both that all true believers will persevere to glorification and that there are none-theless professing believers in the church who receive the Holy Spirit and various spiritual operations that truly affect such people. Many temporary believers have passionately sung a rousing hymn and felt spiritually uplifted by the truths confessed by their lips. They have given money to the church and fed the poor. Were their hearts affected by the Spirit? Yes and no. Ultimately, while we believe credible professions, Spirit-wrought professions prove themselves over time. Indeed, with enough time, all will be made clear concerning the true children of God (Rom. 8:19).

Differences among Believers

What, then, are the differences between true believers and those who are not joined by a real, permanent union with Christ?

The fruit brought forth by temporaries is not true fruit, though it may appear to be fruit. In Hosea's time, this was especially the case:

> Israel is a luxuriant vine
>> that yields its fruit.
> The more his fruit increased,
>> the more altars he built;
> as his country improved,
>> he improved his pillars.
> Their heart is false;
>> now they must bear their guilt.
> The LORD will break down their altars
>> and destroy their pillars. (Hos. 10:1–2)

Israel is described as a "luxuriant vine that yields its fruit." Before that, in Hosea 9, Ephraim was labeled as "stricken"; "their root is dried up; they shall bear no fruit" (Hos. 9:16). Whereas in chapter 9 "fruit" refers to physical progeny, the idea in chapter 10 is more the material prosperity of Israel. Sadly, as God multiplied Israel's fruits, Israel wasted its gifts from above. As God blessed Israel, Israel in turn cursed God. This imagery is likely behind Christ's words in John 15. Israel's prosperity led to sin, not righteousness. Therefore, the people were disciplined (see John 15:2, 6). Yes, they had "fruit," but it was, in God's eyes, an empty vine.

The chief difference between those who truly belong to Christ and those who only appear to belong is in the nature of their faith and fruit. The work of the Spirit brings forth fruit from the person of true faith: "But the fruit of the Spirit is love, joy, peace, patience, kindness, goodness, faithfulness, gentleness, self-control" (Gal. 5:22–23). "Likewise, my brothers," Paul also observes in Romans, "you also have died to the law through the body of Christ, so that you may belong to another, to him who has been raised from the dead, in order that we may bear fruit for God" (Rom. 7:4). These later expressions agree with the earlier testimony of John the Baptist, who maintained that God's people were to "bear fruits in keeping with repentance" (Luke 3:8). As Jesus later made clear, a tree that fails to bring forth good fruit will be "cut down and thrown into the fire" (v. 9).

Our spiritual duties must be fruitful toward God, not primarily toward ourselves. Temporary believers often do many apparently noble and excellent things, but the end of their "fruit" is themselves. Goodwin warns of such people: "And though the assistance wherewith they are enabled to do what they do is more than their own, yet their ends are no higher than themselves, and so they employ but that assistance God gives them wholly for themselves. Now the end for which a true branch brings forth fruit is, that God might be glorified."[12] Our fruit glorifies God: "By this my Father is glorified, that you bear much fruit and so prove to be my disciples" (John 15:8). The chief end of our fruit is to glorify God (1 Cor. 10:31).

True fruit is based on a true, saving union with Christ. Whatever we do of any value in the Christian life is "in Christ." Thus, Christ emphasizes that to bear true fruit, we must abide in him: "Abide in me, and I in you. As the branch cannot bear fruit by itself, unless it abides in the vine, neither can you, unless you abide in me" (John 15:4). If the final cause of our fruit-bearing is the glory of God, the efficient cause of our fruit-bearing is union with Christ. We are kept by Christ as Shepherd and by God in his fatherly providence. As Goodwin comments, "For as we are to honour the husbandman [God the Father] by making him our end, so also the root [Jesus Christ], by doing all in him and from him."[13] "Temporary believers," says Goodwin, "do all principally for themselves, so also all as from themselves; and as they do not make God their end, so nor Christ their root."[14]

The Christian life demands that we accept that we are spiritually bankrupt in ourselves. Thus, if we are to make any progress

12. Goodwin, *Works*, 3:442.
13. Goodwin, 3:443.
14. Goodwin, 3:443.

in Christlikeness, we must have our strength from him and think and act as he did, namely, with a view to the glory of God (John 17:4). We are to joyfully embrace the words of Christ, "apart from me you can do nothing" (15:5). That is good news to the one who acknowledges that we are not sufficient in ourselves, but that our sufficiency is from God (2 Cor. 3:5).

The unfruitful branches do, in a sense, receive strength from Christ, and perform some good actions that can even be a blessing to others. They invariably resist the Spirit, however, insofar as they allow their pride to win over Christ's honor. They are persistent offenders of the problem that Paul warned the Corinthians about when he asked: "What do you have that you did not receive? If then you received it, why do you boast as if you did not receive it?" (1 Cor. 4:7).

Those who have some "spiritual liveliness" but do not persevere are those who do not take seriously that all is from God. Goodwin notes that all we do is "really and all efficiently from Christ."[15] The believers who do not persevere ultimately produce the fruit in themselves and for themselves because the radical principle of their obedience does not spring forth from saving faith.

Faith necessarily empties us of self-sufficiency because it is the hand that receives all from God through Christ by the Spirit. Living by faith in Christ is a constant reminder to abandon that cursed self-sufficiency that we all possess by nature.

Application

We might be tempted to think that it is altogether impossible to discern between a true and false believer. Indeed, when Christ spoke of his betrayal, the disciples, instead of all proclaiming Judas as the obvious choice, asked, "Is it I, Lord?" (Matt. 26:22).

15. Goodwin, 3:443.

Whatever the nature of the work of the Spirit in Judas's life, he did not ultimately obey from the strength of Christ and for God's glory. And he was eventually exposed. He did not possess a repentance that led to life, but one that, quite literally, led to death.

The spiritual illumination that Judas and others like him possess is not, in the final analysis, a saving work. There may be, as Owen observes, "some glances of the beauty, glory, and excellency of spiritual things" in such people, but they do not possess that "direct, steady, intuitive insight into them which is obtained by grace."[16] The habitual sight of Christ belongs to true believers. Though we do not always, in every thought, think of Christ, we are habitually aware of him. Goodwin offers the example of a man on a journey. So if he is going to Cape Town from Vancouver, he does not necessarily think of Cape Town every second of his journey; but habitually in his thoughts he makes it his aim to journey onward in a certain direction, even if the exact destination is not always uppermost in his mind.

Taking every thought captive in obedience to Christ (2 Cor. 10:5) and always setting the Lord before us (Ps. 16:8) does not mean that in every act (e.g., driving, sleeping) we have distinct thoughts of him; "but," says Goodwin, "at the beginning and entrance of greater actions, he still has such actings and exercise of faith; and also often in the progress he renews them; and in the conclusion, when he hath performed them, he doth sanctify Christ in his heart, by ascribing the praise of all unto him."[17] The person who does this loves Christ for who he is and cannot but have many acts of faith, hope, and love toward him. In the end, Judas did not love to behold the glory of the Lord, and so he was not transformed into his likeness (see 2 Cor. 3:18). The life of faith as a Christian is having constant "looks" to Christ, who is

16. Owen, *Works*, 7:21.
17. Goodwin, *Works*, 3:445.

the source of the believer's spiritual life. We love him as our root from whom every blessing from above flows.

The backslider is the person who has stopped beholding the glory of the Lord, and so his or her looks become less frequent. The apostate is the person who has never had a habitual sight of Christ and loved him for who he is. This person did not have the eyes of saving faith that are necessarily pulled to Christ because saving faith's greatest attraction is the one from whom we received such a gift. So while there may be periods of infrequent looks (i.e., backsliding), saving faith will always return to that habitual sight of him that characterizes true children of God.

For Further Reflection

1. What are the marks of true saving faith?
2. What are the different types of "believers"?
3. How can we keep our faith strong?
4. How can we avoid speaking too quickly or confidently about different people related to the good or bad spiritual condition that we see in them?
5. Read and meditate on Hosea 10; Matthew 13:1–23, 47–50; John 15; Romans 11:17–24.

[handwritten notes: not self-sufficient, fruit the glorifying God (for His glory)]

[handwritten notes: abandon self-sufficiency, self-glory. We are spiritually bankrupt apart from Christ (John 15:5) (cf. Hos 10) set eyes/heart on Christ]

4

The Insidiousness of Sin

A declining believer may have sunk so deeply into a state of mere formality, as to substitute the outward and the public means of grace for a close and secret walk with God. (Octavius Winslow)[1]

Drifting

Cyclists almost always enjoy the part of their ride when they, especially after a long climb, begin to drift downward and coast. Drifting downhill in a race is often smart and well deserved. But the Christian race does not allow for drifting until heaven, when our glorious resurrection bodies, perfect in holiness, will know no weakness or suffering but only perfect, powerful, and perpetual freedom in the Spirit.

Don Carson speaks of the propensity of sin toward drifting. Preachers and theologians often use the phrase *insidiousness of sin* to speak of the gradual and often elusive harm that sin brings into our lives. Our inclination toward spiritual drifting away from

---

1. Octavius Winslow, *Personal Declension and Revival of Religion in the Soul* (Eugene, OR: Wipf and Stock, 2001), 18.

Christ manifests the insidiousness of sin. Christian living demands continual effort because, as Carson observes: "People do not drift toward holiness. Apart from grace-driven effort, people do not gravitate toward godliness, prayer, and obedience to Scripture, faith, and delight in the Lord." In fact, in our sinful drifting we dress up our actions or nonactions with false virtues:

> We drift toward compromise and call it tolerance;
>> we drift toward disobedience and call it freedom;
>> we drift toward superstition and call it faith.
> We cherish the indiscipline of lost self-control and call it relaxation;
>> we slouch toward prayerlessness and delude ourselves into thinking we have escaped legalism;
>> we slide toward godlessness and convince ourselves we have been liberated.[2]

Sin loves to drift away from God, and as we move away from him the momentum of sin picks up at an alarming rate. The fact that true saving grace in the soul is indestructible and will always lead to victory does not mean that we should think that gradual decline in our state of grace cannot happen. As Thomas Watson says: "I grant, true Believers, though they do not fall away actually, and lose all their Grace, yet their Grace may fail in the degree, and they may make a great Breach upon their Sanctification. Grace may be *moritura*, not *mortua*, dying but not dead."[3] Nevertheless, Satan will have as much success going to heaven and pushing Christ off his throne than that a true child of God will be lost. But Satan does not give up in his

---

2. D. A. Carson, *For the Love of God: A Daily Companion for Discovering the Riches of God's Word*, vol. 2 (Wheaton, IL: Crossway, 2006), 49.

3. Thomas Watson, *A Body of Practical Divinity* [...] (London: Thomas Parkhurst, 1692), 219.

assaults on Christians, for he is not omniscient and does not infallibly know who is elect and who is not. Therefore, he strikes at as many as he can.

Many mysteries in the Christian life reveal to us the inscrutability of God's ways (Rom. 11:33), which are not our ways (Isa. 55:8–9). Why God allows his children to drift, slip, grow lukewarm, and the like seems hard to understand. Just as we cannot understand why there is so much evil in the world, it may be that we wonder why God doesn't make us a lot more holy than we are.

Without looking too closely at all the causes of backsliding and apostasy, we need to reckon with the fact of sin's insidiousness in the life of the individual Christian as well as in the life of churches. The gradual, often secret, manner of sin taking a foothold in one's life is an ever-present danger that sometimes reveals itself with full-blown apostasy. Archibald Alexander explains well the gravity of the issue because, in the case of apostates, insidious sins begin the process of complete falling away: "they are overcome by some insidious lust or passion, and fall into the habitual practice of some sin, which at first they secretly indulge, but after awhile cast off all disguise, and show to all that they are enslaved by some hurtful and hateful iniquity."[4]

Still, some hide their habitual indulgence (e.g., substance abuse in the drunkard) in the most deceitful and desperate way possible as they seek, in their pride, to mask their sin at all costs. Even in the case of religious people in the church who are unregenerate, they often do not parade their sin from the beginning, but allow it, unopposed, to do its secret work before it becomes public apostasy. Therefore, Christians must take seriously the insidiousness of sin.

4. Archibald Alexander, *Thoughts on Religious Experience* (Philadelphia: Presbyterian Board of Publication, 1841), 205.

Incipient Personal Declension

Octavius Winslow speaks of incipient declension as a "decay of spiritual life and grace in the believer which marks its earliest and more concealed stage."[5] In a sense, we can speak of incipient declension as backsliding in its embryonic stage. It is not obvious, but that is what makes it so dangerous. In fact, this decline is a type of spiritual disease that "may be advanced in the soul so secretly, so silently, and so unobservedly, that the subject of it may have lost much ground, may have parted with many graces and much vigor, and may have been beguiled into an alarming state of spiritual barrenness and decay, before even a suspicion of his real condition has been awakened in his breast."[6]

Like a cancer, sin is often insidious. Sin thrives on working in a subtle manner to go undetected before it is too late. The person who begins to decline does not suddenly lose faith in Christ, which is impossible for the true child of God. But distinct acts of faith, which have Christ as their object, begin to wane and decline. And when these acts of faith decline, sin encroaches by degrees. Thomas Manton observes how Satan "will draw us from motions to actions, and then to hardness in sin and reckless repetition of it!"[7] How does one get to this stage? Manton adds: "Sin gains upon man by insensible degrees."[8] It is a great blessing from God when he restrains sin's insidiousness in our lives. But we must also fight back rather than presume upon God to always restrain sin's insidiousness. Thomas Brooks, in his classic work *Precious Remedies against Satan's Devices*, exhorts believers who wish to not be outwitted by Satan to "make present resistance against

5. Winslow, *Personal Declension*, 15.

6. Winslow, 15.

7. Thomas Manton, *A Practical Commentary or Exposition on the General Epistle of James*, abr. and ed. the Rev. T. M. Macdonogh (London: W. H. Dalton, 1844), 37.

8. Manton, 37.

his first motions; it is safe to resist, it is dangerous to dispute. Eve disputes, and falls in paradise . . . ; Job resists, and conquers upon the dunghill."[9]

As we have a healthy life of faith in Christ, we are living in the Spirit, for the Spirit's work is to glorify the Son in our lives. To the degree that we are looking to Christ, which is to live in the Spirit, we will be sensitive to the evil, danger, and guilt of sin. We will be best equipped to put up our spiritual defenses against the ever-present danger of sin's relentless pursuit against us.

Our lack of sensitivity to the evil, danger, and guilt of sin allows sin to do its work. As this occurs, our eyes are diverted from Christ, and we become desensitized to sin. We become like the false prophets in Jeremiah's time and speak, "Peace, peace" to our own souls, "when there is no peace" (Jer. 8:11). We forsake God, "the fountain of living waters," for "broken cisterns" (2:13), but we are unaware that the sludge we are drinking is slowly going to kill us if we are not careful to repent. Our evil will catch up with us like the sweet-tasting ethylene glycol of antifreeze that poisons to death those who unknowingly drink it. But this happens because as we look away from Christ, we are also abandoning a healthy fear of God: "the fear of me is not in you" (2:19).

While this may be a sensitive discussion for some, those who gain considerable weight because of gluttony do not go from a healthy frame to obesity overnight. It is usually gradual. Whether because of gluttony, a genetic disposition, poor diet, medications, or some other reason, when people gain weight, the shock is more evident to those who saw them at their healthy weight and then saw them again months or years later at their unhealthy weight. The change simply manifests a pattern that developed over time. Backsliding is like unhealthy weight gain. In fact, unhealthy weight

9. Thomas Brooks, *Precious Remedies against Satan's Devices* [. . .] (Philadelphia: Jonathan Pounder, 1810), 312.

gain may even reveal a spiritual drifting from the Lord through indulgence of fleshly desires for something good, yet without self-control (like abusing alcohol). It is often due to changes of pattern, and slowly but surely the problem becomes obvious over time. Good habits are replaced with bad habits.

The slow, steady, and surreptitious way of backsliding has caught up with many Christians who felt the powerful temptation to drift a little, which soon became drifting a lot. God sometimes brings us into what John Owen calls a "season of unusual outward prosperity."[10] Just as we naturally love to drift, so we also love prosperity. But with it come many types of powerful temptations. Indeed, as Owen remarks, "prosperity is a temptation, many temptations, and that because, without eminent supplies of grace, it is apt to cast a soul into a frame and temper exposed to any temptation, and provides it with fuel and food for all. It has provision for lust and darts for Satan."[11] Prosperity and ease are fuels for temptations to enter and harm the soul. Sin's insidiousness often lives off outward prosperity.

Personal declension, through sin's insidiousness, regularly happens through inward temptations that are not mortified. We should not underestimate the power of indwelling sin that remains in believers. Owen speaks of "an exceeding efficacy and power in the remainders of indwelling sin in believers, with a constant working towards evil."[12] He later explains how indwelling sin is "effectually operative in rebelling and inclining to evil, when the will of doing good is in a particular manner active and inclining unto obedience."[13] This explains why sin so easily creeps in—even when we are doing our best, sin is doing its worst. Thus, as Owen

10. John Owen, *The Works of John Owen*, ed. W. H. Goold, 24 vols. (Edinburgh: T&T Clark, 1850–53), 6:127.
   11. Owen, 6:127.
   12. Owen, 6:159.
   13. Owen, 6:161.

famously said, "be killing sin or it will be killing you."[14] As Christ crushed the head of the serpent, we are to take fresh blows to our sin each day in the Spirit (Rom. 8:13). There are three certainties in life: death, taxes, and indwelling sin working hard.

The root of personal, incipient declension, of all backsliding, is unbelief, which is the first and worst sin. Adam and Eve sinned in their unbelief; they did not believe God's word (Gen. 3:1, 4). Pride resulted from unbelief, as they wished to become like God (v. 5).

Jesus marveled at two things in particular: the faith of the Roman centurion (Matt. 8:10) and the unbelief of his own people in Nazareth (Mark 6:6). Once we stop living by faith, trusting God each day, we will inevitably backslide. "Unbelief," remarks Owen, "sets all the corrupt lusts and affections of the heart at liberty to act according to their own perverse nature and inclination."[15] Even for those with true saving faith, a great deal of unbelief wages war against their souls. We can say that we believe, but we can also say that we hate our unbelief. Like the father of the convulsing son, we need to continually cry out to the Lord, "I believe; help my unbelief!" (Mark 9:24). Unbelief remains at the heart of our sin and our love for sin. We even, to some extent, enjoy our unbelief because living by faith is not an easy way at times. Living by faith is hard. Ask Abraham; ask Samson; ask David; ask Peter!

We need to be reminded that the life of faith is always the better way, even if it is a painful way at times. Believing that it is better to love one's enemy or turn the other cheek is not easy. We quickly and easily descend into the realm of unbelief because the demands of the life of faith are sometimes very difficult. The Puritan John Ball confesses in his excellent work on faith: "O Lord, I am grossly ignorant of your ways, doubtful of your truth, distrustful of your power and goodness, disobedient to your commandments. You

---

14. Owen, 6:9.
15. Owen, 21:123.

have given rare and excellent promises in your holy Word, but I inquire not after them, rejoice not in them, cleave not unto them in truth and steadfastness, settle not my heart upon them, make them not my own, keep them not safe."[16] Faith opens up the door to God's promises, but very often we only, through willful ignorance, fail to open the door fully to all that God has promised.

The sin of unbelief is exceedingly serious, since it gives birth to other sins and aims to cast out all progress in grace. Unbelief attacks our virtues and weakens them. Unbelief picks us up and carries us away from God. This grieves God and Christ because they know the power of unbelief on the soul. Remember that on the road to Emmaus, Jesus is grieved by his disciples' unbelief: "And he said to them, 'O foolish ones, and slow of heart to believe all that the prophets have spoken!'" (Luke 24:25). After that, Jesus appears to the Eleven and again questions their unbelief: "And he said to them, 'Why are you troubled, and why do doubts arise in your hearts?'" (v. 38). He practically chastises Thomas for believing only because he has seen the risen Christ (John 20:29).

Living by faith keeps us from being hardened by sin's deceitfulness (Heb. 3:13). Sin deceives us so that when we begin to slide from God, we are sometimes betrayed into thinking that we are not slipping. The Laodiceans were deceived about their spiritual state (Rev. 3:17). Stephen Charnock wisely stated that "nothing is so natural as heart-deceit and presumptuous confidence. . . . Self-flattery is one of the strongest branches which grows upon the pride of nature. How vain is it to fancy to yourselves a fitness for heaven, while there are only preparations for hell?"[17] True saving faith humbles us and keeps us from self-flattery because faith looks to Christ, who is the Savior of real sinners. We are both emptied and filled when we believe: emptied of self and filled with Christ.

16. John Ball, *A Treatise of Faith* [. . .] (London: For Edward Brewster, 1657), 202.
17. Stephen Charnock, *The Complete Works of Stephen Charnock*, 5 vols. (Edinburgh: James Nichol, 1864–66; repr., Edinburgh: Banner of Truth, 1985), 3:63.

We cannot, then, overstate the importance of true faith in the battle against backsliding. As Charles Spurgeon once pointed out, "Faith is like Samson's hair but on the Christian; cut it off, and you may put out his eyes—and he can do nothing."[18] Before we can begin to appreciate the value of faith, we must understand the heinousness of unbelief. Then and only then can we desire the remedy. And let us be clear about one thing: this is not a matter that should unsettle only unbelievers. As believers, we should be deeply concerned about our unbelief and the duty placed on us to rest more and more on the one who is "Faithful and True" (Rev. 19:11).

Incipient (Corporate) Declension

Prosperity, outward blessings, and the like can be exceedingly dangerous not only for a Christian, but also for a church. The people in the church of Laodicea boasted of their prosperity. Jesus cautioned them: "For you say, I am rich, I have prospered, and I need nothing, not realizing that you are wretched, pitiable, poor, blind, and naked" (Rev. 3:17). Clearly, they were unaware of their backsliding and needed a thunderous rebuke from the Lord of glory. Corporate sin was on display.

Before the church in Laodicea and after its example, churches have been crippled by the insidious nature of sin. The apostles founded churches and instructed their people in the great mysteries of the gospel. Paul planted the church in Corinth, and not long (perhaps several years) after his planting they were up to all sorts of nonsense. He preached the gospel in its purity to the Galatians, but they too found themselves trapped in the worst of evils: legalism. Indeed, readers of the New Testament letters cannot help but feel that many of the churches addressed are on

18. Charles H. Spurgeon, "The Sin of Unbelief: A Sermon Delivered on Sunday Morning, January 14, 1855," in *The New Park Street Pulpit Sermons* (London: Passmore & Alabaster, 1855), 1:202.

precarious ground. We must ask ourselves whether we can take anything for granted when we do not have Christ and the apostles speaking directly to our problems.

Now, the issue before us is not so much that churches very often decline over a time, but that this declension happens in a manner that leaves many in the church unaware that something is amiss. Each Lord's Day when Christ's glories are not exalted, when no duties are pressed on those who are called and enabled to be slaves of righteousness, and when the Word of God is eclipsed by man's words is a day when God's people regress, perhaps even in ignorance. True, some courageously seek reformation of such churches, but they usually fight a losing battle and are regarded by the godless as agitators who are overconcerned with theology instead of love.

Whole denominations also decline, but they do not go from powerful gospel proclamations to outright liberalism in the space of a few months. Slowly but surely, for various reasons, small changes here and there lead to bigger changes here and there. False teachers are not dealt with as they should be, and Satan's secret methods take hold of pastors and flocks. The morality of the world begins to set the terms for the church. Naturally, it should be the other way around, but who can deny that the church has often fallen into the trap of appeasing worldly values? The "woke" values of the world are shaping entire churches, not just individuals.

Christians must be careful concerning their immediate local-church context. Awareness of the incipient downward progression of those around you because of a failure from the pulpit is not easy to discern. Unbelief has corporate effects. The growing unbelief of a father in a Christian household can and does lead to backsliding among his family members. Unbelief spreads like a plague. In Noah's day, the world turned a deaf ear to his preaching. He was "a herald of righteousness" (2 Peter 2:5), but evidently no one saw the need to escape the coming judgment. The prevailing sin of

God's people in the exodus was unbelief (Ps. 95:7–8; Heb. 3), and so they died in the wilderness (Num. 26:65). Those miraculously redeemed out of Egypt could not enter the promised land because of unbelief (Heb. 3:19). We are speaking not about an individual here and there, but sometimes of thousands of those who counted themselves among God's people (cf. 1 Cor. 10:6–10).

Application

How did God keep Christ from backsliding? How did he keep Christ from allowing sin into his life for even a second? The author of Hebrews tells us that although Christ "was a son, he learned obedience through what he suffered" (Heb. 5:8). The Man of Sorrows was a Man of Suffering. Outward prosperity and ease were not characteristics of Christ's life: "Foxes have holes, and birds of the air have nests, but the Son of Man has nowhere to lay his head" (Matt. 8:20).

The Father ordered Christ's life circumstances, just as he does ours. The circumstances of Christ's life forced him to continually live by faith. As Owen comments on Hebrews 2:13 ("I will put my trust in him"), "In all the troubles and difficulties that he had to contend withal, he put his trust in God."[19] As one like his brothers (Heb. 2:11–18), Christ was always required to live by faith in the "care and protection of God."[20] The many and varied sufferings he underwent were the trial of his faith, but the trial of his faith is what strengthened his trust in God so that he would not slip back even once (see 10:38, "but my righteous one shall live by faith, and if he shrinks back, my soul has no pleasure in him").

What will keep sin from gaining a foothold in your life and deceiving you that all is well when in fact all is not well? Living

19. Owen, *Works*, 20:429.
20. Owen, 20:429.

by faith. But this is not meant to be a pious platitude. The life of faith is coupled with a life with many difficulties. Faith answers to life's problems. When we are free from any distresses, anxieties, or sufferings, we tend to slip. God, as a gracious Father, not only grants us the gift of faith, but providentially provides a context whereby our faith will get to work by looking to God and Christ in times of distress. These distresses keep us from deception and falling into sinful patterns. Many may turn to drugs and alcohol in times of suffering instead of thinking that maybe a season of suffering will yield much fruit if we patiently wait on the Lord.

Not only are we to keep up direct acts of faith toward God and Christ each day, but we must resist those small inclinations to evil that arise in our hearts. The smallest sin in the world cannot be tolerated. For example, perhaps you do not cruise the internet for pornography, but you easily tolerate content on cable and internet media that is becoming more and more illicit. You think nothing of the second look with desire you give to that scene, image, or reel about sex topics that are unsuitable to be spoken about. Yet this is where we must exercise greater diligence now rather than later. When we begin to tolerate small sins in our souls, we are opening the door to bigger sins, which, like unwanted guests coming to an out-of-control high school party, care nothing for the owner of the house.

Finally, corporately we must deal with all sorts of individuals living together as part of a body. The less wealthy may struggle with envy toward those who are wealthy. But the wealthy may struggle with a dependence on possessions instead of God. The Laodiceans were a wealthy congregation, but they were in fact poor (Rev. 3:17). Corporate declension can happen for many different reasons. Doctrinally, churches can go off the path, but issues of envy, pride, and other such sins often speed along the doctrinal infidelity to our Savior. Sin sneaks in and Christ sneaks out, sometimes without churches' even being aware of what has happened.

For Further Reflection

1. How does this chapter help us to view suffering in the life of a believer?
2. If unbelief can affect those around us, what does this say about our life of faith?
3. How do acts of faith toward God and Christ help keep us from backsliding?
4. Think of a time in your life when you manifested the reality of John Owen's maxim: "Be killing sin or it will be killing you."
5. Read and meditate on Psalm 95; Mark 6:1–6; Hebrews 2:11–18.

5

The Coldness of Love

All who do not love God are strangers and antichrists. They might come to the churches, but they cannot be numbered among the children of God. (Augustine)[1]

Growing Cold

In any truly loving relationship, a great deal of sadness usually ensues when one person stops loving the other, especially when there is apparently no good reason for the change of heart. The Bible offers us many such cases of God's people's turning from their love for him. In times of persecution and wickedness, as Jesus says in Matthew 24:12, "the love of many will grow cold." Sadly, many will determine that it is not worth it to endure suffering to persevere to the end.

In Jeremiah's time, God commanded the prophet to proclaim in Jerusalem the faithlessness of God's people, aggravated by the divine recollection, "I remember the devotion of your youth, your

1. Augustine, "Homilies on the First Epistle of John," in *Nicene and Post-Nicene Fathers*, ed. Philip Schaff (Grand Rapids: Eerdmans, 1956), 7:503.

love as a bride" (Jer. 2:2). God chastised them for abandoning their love for the one who had gloriously redeemed them.

In the New Testament, our Lord in a similar manner rebukes the people of the Ephesian church because they had abandoned the love they had at first (Rev. 2:4). This may well include their loss of evangelistic zeal—but losing such zeal reveals leaving their love of Christ, since the highest aim of evangelism is the glory of Christ. He therefore calls on them to repent and return to their former love (i.e., zeal for others), which was really a return to loving Christ.

The sad reality cannot be ignored: love can wane and "grow cold" not only in human relationships but also in the relationship that professing Christians have with the triune God. But this raises several important questions about the nature of true love, what causes it to grow cold, and what can be done to recapture our first love.

What Is Love?

Backsliders whose faith weakens will inevitably find that their love weakens toward God and toward man. William Ames rightfully argued that faith, not love, "is the first foundation of the spiritual building of man. This is so not only because faith is the beginning, but also because it sustains and holds together all the parts of the building. It has the nature of a root in that it gives power to bring forth fruit."[2] You cannot have a strong faith and a weak love. A strong faith begets a strong love; a weak faith begets a weak love.

While faith is the first foundation, the great mark of the Christian faith is love (Deut. 6:4–5; Matt. 22:34–40; Rom. 13:8). Christians have a "vertical love" toward God and a "horizontal

2. William Ames, *The Marrow of Theology*, ed. and trans. John Dykstra Eusden (1968; repr., Grand Rapids: Baker, 1997), 250.

love" toward man. The latter is often the best indicator of whether there is a vertical love at all (Matt. 25:45; 1 John 4:20–21). When backsliding begins, love wanes not only toward God but also toward man.

Love is a fruit of the Spirit, a virtue that seeks union, satisfaction, and goodwill. Peter Lombard, one of the great theologians of the medieval church, noted that "charity is the love by which God is loved for his own sake, and our neighbor is loved for the sake of God or in God."[3] Ultimately, all true love is directed to God in one way or another: (1) directly, such as in our corporate worship; or (2) indirectly, as when we feed the poor.

Love, as the old theologians noted, has three basic components that give us a fuller picture of the biblical concept of true love. True love, according to Ames, leads to a "love of union, of satisfaction or contentment, and good will."[4] These are the so-called parts of love. Understanding love in this way has many advantages. But most especially, it explains how God's love to us is not merely one-way but reaches its goal of reciprocation.

In the love of union, we see how, even before the foundation of the world, God chose us to be in Christ (Eph. 1:4). This union has been called *predestinarian union*; it is an *immanent* work of God in eternity. Thus, when Christ lives, dies, and is raised from the dead, he is acting not only for himself but for his people—even people yet to be born who are his. We are united with him in his life, death, and resurrection. This has been called a *transient* work of God toward us (Rom. 6:3–5). Finally, our union with Christ reaches its goal when we, by the Spirit, believe and are joined to Christ (Eph. 1:13–14). God applies the merits of Christ to us, but only through faith alone can we receive these merits. While these

---

3. Peter Lombard, *The Sentences*, bk. 3, *On the Incarnation of the Word*, trans. Giulio Silano, Mediaeval Sources in Translation 45 (Toronto: Pontifical Institute of Mediaeval Studies, 2010), 113.

4. Ames, *Marrow of Theology*, 250.

concepts are quite theological, they wonderfully show that the love of union that God shows toward us reveals his love toward us. The triune God identifies himself with us by an unbreakable and eternal union.

Besides the love of union, there is a love of satisfaction. As Christians, we possess eternal life, which is to know the only true God and Jesus Christ (John 17:3). Knowing God satisfies us. As we learn of his attributes, we should grow in our affection and satisfaction toward the triune God. We learn that only he can truly and eternally satisfy us. But this satisfaction that we have in him arises out of the satisfaction that he has in us. God delights in his people. This cannot be emphasized enough because backsliders typically have trouble overcoming the doubt that their heavenly Father could possibly continue to delight in them. But God delights in the good that he has bestowed on us. He cannot but delight in the image of Christ that is in us. The love of satisfaction is therefore reciprocal. God loves us with a delight that we must return toward him.

Finally, there is a love of goodwill. As Christians, we are worshipers of God; we offer him glory, honor, and praise. We are devoted to our Father in all things, just as our Savior was during his ministry on earth (John 8:29). In living for God in love, we are simply responding to his loving goodwill toward us whereby he grants us good gifts from above (Ps. 85:12; John 3:27; 1 Cor. 4:7; James 1:17). There is a never-ending granting of good things from above toward those who are in Christ. As we meditate on the good that the Lord has shown to us, how can we not respond in offering our praise, love, and affection? But, alas, we do grow cold, and one reason we do is that we forget to think on God's goodness toward us.

To the degree that we behold the glory of God in the face of Jesus Christ, we will love God. Our union with Christ will lead to a love that has both satisfaction and goodwill toward God.

Our ability to express such love is not from ourselves, of course, but we are lovers of God because the Spirit, who dwells in us, is a Spirit of love. As Jonathan Edwards insisted in his justly famous book *Charity and Its Fruits*: "The Spirit of God is a Spirit of love, and when the former enters the soul, love also enters with it. God is love, and he that has God dwelling in him by his Spirit, will have love dwelling in him also."[5] God is love, and because he is a relational God toward his people, we are to respond to the God of love with love. God loves his Son; so must we. In fact, we are never more like God than when we love his Son. And God, being rich in mercy, does not leave us without many reasons to love Jesus Christ—a love involving affection with a commitment to self-sacrifice for the one who sacrificed his life for us (John 15:13; 1 John 4:9–11; 3:16).

Love of the World

Before we look at the specific symptoms of backsliding and apostasy—such as prayerlessness, infrequent corporate worship, and so on—we need to understand a powerful driving force that allures us away from our love for God: the world. When the world clings to our souls, "it not only hinders the shining lustre of [our] graces, but by degrees it cankers them," notes Thomas Watson.[6]

Octavius Winslow perceptively remarked concerning love of the world in relation to backsliding that "no two affections can be more opposite and antagonist than love to God and love to the world: it is impossible that they can both exist with equal force in the same breast; the one or the other must be supreme,—they

5. Jonathan Edwards, *Charity and Its Fruits*, ed. Tryon Edwards (Philadelphia: Presbyterian Board of Publication, 1874), 4.

6. Thomas Watson, *A Divine Cordial: Or, the Transcendent Priviledge of Those That Love God* (London, 1831), 107–8.

cannot occupy the same throne."[7] As our Lord stated, "No one can serve two masters, for either he will hate the one and love the other, or he will be devoted to the one and despise the other" (Matt. 6:24). Hence the apostle James writes: "You adulterous people! Do you not know that friendship with the world is enmity with God? Therefore whoever wishes to be a friend of the world makes himself an enemy of God" (James 4:4).

In *Precious Remedies against Satan's Devices*, Thomas Brooks explains how Satan presents the world in "beauty and bravery" to turn us from God.[8] Brooks sadly exclaims: "Ah! How many professors in these days have for a time followed hard after God, Christ, and ordinances, till the devil has set before them the world in all its beauty and bravery, which has bewitched them first to have low thoughts of holy things, and then to be cold in their affections to them, and then to slight them; and at last, with the young man in the gospel, to turn their backs upon them."[9] "Where one thousand is destroyed by the world's frowns," observes Brooks, "ten thousand are destroyed by its smiles. The world . . . kisses us, and betrays us, like Judas. . . . The honour, splendour, and all the glory of this world, are but sweet poisons, that will much endanger us, if they do not eternally destroy us."[10] In the words of Brooks, Christians can turn away from "following hard" after the Lord in love, to pursue the world with the same zeal. Yet with such fervor the Christian cannot follow both the Lord and the world at the same time as though pursuing two masters.

The warnings about the pull of the world are many in God's Word. But few are as clear as from the apostle John's pen. In his

---

7. Octavius Winslow, *Personal Declension and Revival of Religion in the Soul* (Eugene, OR: Wipf and Stock, 2001), 75.

8. Thomas Brooks, *Precious Remedies against Satan's Devices* [. . .] (Philadelphia: Jonathan Pounder, 1810), 117.

9. Brooks, 118.

10. Brooks, 118.

letter to Christians, he exhorts them about the dangers of the world and the consequences of putting the world before God: "Do not love the world or the things in the world. If anyone loves the world, the love of the Father is not in him" (1 John 2:15). The stakes for John are evidently high: love of the world means that there is no love of the Father in such a person. He answers why this is so: "For all that is in the world—the desires of the flesh and the desires of the eyes and pride of life—is not from the Father but is from the world" (v. 16). An attraction to the world reveals a heart that has lost or is severely lacking attraction to the things of God. John not only gives the reason why love of the world and love of God cannot coexist in the same heart, but also reminds his hearers why they should not give preeminence to love of the world: "the world is passing away along with its desires, but whoever does the will of God abides forever" (v. 17). There is a warning—a reality check of sorts—and a promise.

The love of the world may include things that are explicitly sinful. The world presents us with many sinful allurements, such as pornography, illicit drugs, and vain philosophies. Yet the world also contains many things that are not sinful in themselves, but because of the waywardness of the human heart good things become bad things. So fine wine and aged cheese may be good, but gorging oneself with them in drunkenness and gluttony is not. The former problems are obvious to most Christians, but the latter are less so.

The attainment or pursuit of wealth does not need to be sinful, but obvious dangers are associated with such pursuits. As Paul warns: "For the love of money is a root of all kinds of evils. It is through this craving that some have wandered away from the faith and pierced themselves with many pangs" (1 Tim. 6:10). Many have, in the pursuit of wealth, put themselves at risk physically, emotionally, and ultimately spiritually. To gain worldly wealth, many have abandoned time with their children, spouse, and corporate worship. They have stopped trusting God and have said, rather, "My will be done." Usually they pretend that forsaking time with their family or missing church is only temporary, but we can never expect to be blessed by God for a season of so-called temporary sin. Are we able to put a time limit on a season in which we say that we will neglect essential duties but promise to make sure that it won't last?

The pursuit of wealth on our terms instead of God's terms usually means that other areas of our lives are not functioning as they ought. We pursue wealth sinfully when that pursuit leads to our failing to give our offerings to the work of the kingdom. The kingdom always comes first. When Jesus exhorts us to "seek first the kingdom of God" (Matt. 6:33), we would do well to look at the context of those words!

When John says that love of the world includes "the desires of the flesh" (1 John 2:16), he uses a word for "desire" that is found almost forty times in the New Testament and almost always has negative connotations. The heart (desire) is what leads us astray in this world. So "the desires of the eyes" (v. 16) refers to the problem of covetousness, which explains the next words, "pride of life." The pride of life includes things such as possessions and goods: "But if anyone has the world's goods and sees his brother in need, yet closes his heart against him, how does God's love abide in him?" (3:17). Possessions and goods can easily puff us up and cause our hearts to swell with pride so that love for God is extinguished.

Andrew Fuller warns of covetousness—desiring for yourself what belongs to someone else—in his comments on 1 John 2:15. He asserts that this specific sin will, "in all probability, prove the eternal overthrow of more characters among professing people, than almost any other sin; and this because it is almost the only sin which may be indulged, and a profession of religion at the same time supported."[11] Naturally, covetousness can manifest

---

11. Andrew Fuller, *The Backslider* (London: Hamilton, Adams, and Co., 1840), 26.

itself in obvious ways by how we speak and how we act in relation to our words. But covetousness can also hide easily in the hearts of people who allow their sinful desires to have free rein there in terms of fantasies.

Besides the pursuit of wealth to have goods and riches, we also have a natural tendency to want to be loved by the people of the world. Now, obviously, Christians should not wish to be hated by anyone. Nor should we doubt our faithfulness if there are non-Christians who love us. But such is our desire to be loved by people that we are often unfaithful toward God. Living as people-pleasers ultimately seeks glory for ourselves that is meant for God alone, which is "vainglory" or that which is empty. In connection with the acknowledgment, approval, and adulation we get from others, Rebecca DeYoung notes, "Glory goes bad when we desire it for the wrong things and for the wrong ends."[12] Indeed, it is antithetical to the Christian life to seek the applause of everyone around us. Jesus made it clear that if the world hated him, it will also hate us who follow him (John 15:18). Likewise, Paul assures us of many things, including the sometimes inconvenient truth that godly living leads to persecution in this world (2 Tim. 3:12).

We also sometimes find that our non-Christian friends have many qualities that we admire and enjoy. Again, spending time with such people need not be sinful, but when we start to surround ourselves more with the people of the world than with the people of God, the inevitable thought patterns, desires, and ideas of those at enmity with God begin to sink into our own souls, even sometimes without our being aware.

Additionally, many professing Christians have willingly entered into romantic relationships with non-Christians, hoping to see

12. Rebecca Konyndyk DeYoung, *Vainglory: The Forgotten Vice* (Grand Rapids: Eerdmans, 2014), 26.

these people eventually change allegiances to Christ ("missionary dating"). While occasionally God shows mercy and brings about a conversion of such an unbeliever, very often the believer is the one who drifts away from the Lord rather than the nonbeliever's drifting into the kingdom. Paul's general principle in 2 Corinthians 6:14–18 ("Do not be unequally yoked with unbelievers") has direct application to the practice of relationships between a believer and an unbeliever. When one has God as a Father and the other has the devil, an encroachment of darkness will often lead the believer away from loving the Lord.

Sometimes our love for the world leads us to avoid persecution in its various forms. Paul regrets the action of Demas, who, "in love with this present world, has deserted me and gone to Thessalonica" (2 Tim. 4:10). Demas had been at one time a loyal coworker with Paul (Col. 4:14; Philem. 24). Then he deserted Paul. He loved the world, but specifically what was his problem? The context gives us a clue. Paul speaks of his suffering before mentioning Demas (e.g., 2 Tim. 3:11–12). Demas likely also took his eyes off what is promised, for that is what kept Paul going in times of difficulty: "Henceforth there is laid up for me the crown of righteousness, which the Lord, the righteous judge, will award to me on that day, and not only to me but also to all who have loved his appearing" (4:8). The future promise of glory helps us to withstand the present time of persecution. Demas forgot that and chose love for a fading world over love for an eternal God.

The possessions of the world and the desire for acceptance have robbed many Christians of their first love. They have been allured away by obvious sins (e.g., pornography, drunkenness) and less obvious or more overlooked and tolerated sins (e.g., materialism, excessive work, gluttony, sports, pursuit of leisure). The world wants to suck our love for God out of us. It never rests, always works, and often succeeds.

Application

Watson claims that the lack of love is "the ground of apostasy.
. . . He who has not the love of God rooted in his heart will fall
away in time of temptation. . . . He who has no love in his heart to
God, you may set him down for an apostate."[13] Therefore, make it
your aim to pray continually that you may always love God from
the heart. Anselm of Canterbury prayed:

> My God,
> I pray that I may so know you and love you
> that I may rejoice in you.
> And if I may not do so fully in this life
> let me go steadily on
> to the day when I come to that fullness. . . .
> Meanwhile let my mind meditate on it
> let my heart love it
> let my mouth preach it
> let my soul hunger for it
> my flesh thirst for it
> and my whole being desire it
> until I enter into the joy of my Lord.[14]

Anselm prayed to know and love God and attain everything
related to that. He understood that when we love God, we can
then serve him well. Similarly, Augustine famously stated, "Once
and for all, I give you this one short command: love God, and do
what you will."[15] If God comes first, our actions will be dictated
by the all-consuming desire to serve him and please him.

13. Watson, *Divine Cordial*, 104.
14. Anselm, *Proslogion*, in *Eerdmans' Book of Christian Classics: A Treasury of Christian Writings through the Centuries* (Grand Rapids: Eerdmans, 1985), 27.
15. Augustine, "Homilies on the First Epistle of John," 7:505.

Charles Spurgeon speaks of God's love for us and how we can respond to such love: "As love comes from heaven, so it must feed on heavenly bread. It cannot exist in this wilderness, unless it is nurtured from above, and fed by manna from on high. On what, then, does love feed? Why, it feeds on love. That which brought it forth becomes its food. 'We love him because he first loved us.' The constant motive and sustaining power of our love to God is his love to us."[16] The spiritual diet of the Christian must be the love of God. This can mean that we make good use of his Word and sacraments, for example, but we cannot derive any real benefit from these means that he has appointed if there is not a loving heart that feeds on such love. This may mean that we ought to prepare better, through prayer, not only to receive God's grace but to have a loving heart ready to receive more of God's love.

Besides God's love for us, we are also constrained by the love of Christ. As Paul said, "For the love of Christ controls us, because we have concluded this: that one has died for all, therefore all have died; and he died for all, that those who live might no longer live for themselves but for him who for their sake died and was raised" (2 Cor. 5:14–15). When we, by faith, believe the gospel, we cannot but respond in love—a love that controls us in such a way that we live for Christ, who lived, died, and rose for us.

Finally, we should spend time with those who do love God. As Richard Sibbes wisely stated: "Conversing with sinful, cold people casts a damp upon us. But let us labour, if we will be wise for our own souls, when we find any coldness of affection, to converse with those that have sweet and heavenly affections. It will marvellously work upon our hearts."[17] God uses means to accomplish his ends. To excite our hearts aflame with love for him, he will

16. Charles H. Spurgeon, "Love: A Sermon," in *The New Park Street Pulpit* (London: Passmore & Alabaster, 1894), 5:35.

17. Richard Sibbes, *The Complete Works of Richard Sibbes, D.D.*, 7 vols. (Edinburgh: James Nichol, 1863), 4:197.

often make use of his people in various ways. Those who love the Lord have a marvelous ministry, for their love is often infectious without even knowing it, but sometimes to the end that others are brought back to loving their Savior as they ought.

For Further Reflection

1. How does prayer nurture love for our triune God in terms of union, satisfaction, and goodwill all at the same time?
2. What are some ways that Christians have shown improper love for the world, yet without much response from the church? How do we account for this?
3. We may struggle to show love toward the "unlovely" people in our churches. How does reflecting on the love of Christ help with that struggle?
4. How have others helped you in love to love the Lord and others?
5. Read and meditate on Jeremiah 2; 2 Corinthians 5:11–6:18.

6

The Resurgence of Pride

Augustine is bold in saying, "It is profitable for proud men to fall sometimes into open sin, that they may know and understand themselves." (Thomas Manton)[1]

Pride and Humility

From the very beginning, man was made to serve and obey God, giving him the glory in all things. Our relationship to the Creator can never move beyond one of servanthood and praise (Ps. 150; Luke 17:10). Any service rendered to God was made possible by him, since Adam's faculties and powers were entrusted to him from above (John 3:27).

Adam's sin was a type of self-exaltation whereby he would proclaim independence from God. Unbelief toward God's word (threat) led to pride. Flagrantly disregarding God, Adam desired to be like his Maker. He chose his will over God's. Adam gave up servanthood, which was true freedom, and landed in bondage. In the

---

1. Thomas Manton, *The Complete Works of Thomas Manton*, 22 vols. (London: James Nisbet & Co., 1872), 6:414.

image of God, Adam was designed to bear his likeness while accepting subservience to him. Adam was in himself "poor" because all that he had depended entirely upon another (i.e., God). He committed a type of theft in trying to be like God—a robbery. This "poor" man attempted to become rich on his own terms.

By contrast, the Son of God, who was rich in himself, became poor (2 Cor. 8:9). In humility, Jesus considered others more significant than himself and lived the life of a servant in obedience to God. He did not consider "robbery" as a viable option but willingly made himself nothing (Phil. 2:3–11 KJV). Pride (Adam) was the ruin of humanity, but humility (Christ) was its salvation.

Pride did not stop with Adam. Sadly, not only among the vast multitude of unbelievers, but also among the people of God, pride has cast many souls into terrible dangers. Such displays cause a stench in the nostrils of God instead of the pleasing aroma of humility. This idolatrous determination to be God leads a sinner into direct confrontation and competition with the true and only God. Humility kept Christ close to his Father; pride drives us from him, and consequently each other.

Whatever the specific sin of Satan may have been (e.g., striving for authority), it seems that we are on safe ground in attributing pride as the cause of his departure from God (1 Tim. 3:6). This sin has infected (fallen) angels and humans to the extent that basically all sins are in one way or another connected to this monstrous evil. Augustine argued in *The City of God* that pride is the beginning of sin, and "what is pride but the craving for undue exaltation? And this is undue exaltation, when the soul abandons Him to whom it ought to cleave as its end, and becomes a kind of end to itself."[2] Pride leads to abandoning him who should be the one whom we should most wish to cling to. In the medieval church, pride was commonly

---

2. Augustine, *The City of God*, trans. Marcus Dods (Loschberg, Germany: Jazzybee Verlag, 2015), 314.

viewed as the root of all sin, specifically the capital sins such as vainglory, envy, sloth, avarice, wrath, lust, and gluttony. As Rebecca DeYoung notes, medieval theologians used images to describe the foundational role of pride, with some likening it to the queen of sin, the commander-in-chief over the army of sin, and the root and trunk from which the branches and fruit of all other sins grow.[3]

Pride affects not just individuals (2 Chron. 32:24–26), but groups of people (Gen. 11:4) and churches (1 Cor. 1:26–30). It began in heaven with Satan but now abounds on earth. The pavement that leads many people to eternal perdition is pride. But there are also professing Christians who allow pride to gain a foothold in their walk that leads them away from the path of righteousness. Henry Scougal laments that we are all naturally proud and that "we have a high esteem of ourselves, and would have every body else to value and esteem us. This disease is very deeply rooted in our corrupt nature."[4] The effects of this sin are exceedingly dangerous: "Pride alone," says Scougal, "is the source and foundation of almost all the disorders in the world, of all our troubles, and of all our sins."[5] It not only draws us from God but is our attempt to fight him.

We should be acutely aware of the connection between pride and backsliding. John Prideaux, Bishop of Worcester and Regius Professor of Divinity at Oxford, in a sermon on backsliding, made the point that there is "nothing so dangerous to the estate of a Christian, that travails here from Egypt to the heavenly Canaan, as spiritual pride, and carnal security."[6] The backslider is necessarily a proud person.

3. Rebecca Konyndyk DeYoung, *Glittering Vices: A New Look at the Seven Deadly Sins and Their Remedies*, 2nd ed. (Grand Rapids: Brazos Press, 2020), 26, 30–31, 34.

4. Henry Scougal, *Works of the Rev. Henry Scougal* (Glasgow: William Collins, 1830), 171.

5. Scougal, 171.

6. John Prideaux, *Ephesus Backsliding: Considered and Applied to These Times* [. . .] (Oxford: Leonard Lichfield, 1636), 1.

Paul's Warning to the Gentiles

For all the beautiful promises contained in the book of Romans, especially in chapter 8, we cannot forget the section whereby Paul warns Gentile Christians of the danger of spiritual pride (see Rom. 11:17–24). The discussion of pride occurs in the context of backsliding and apostasy. The language in Romans 11 is not without precedent.

In Jeremiah's time, the prophet was told more than once not to pray for his people (Jer. 7:16; 11:14). The people of God, caught up in idolatry, thought that they could receive help both from their idols and from God. A sort of spiritual pride was present whereby they wanted religion on their terms, not God's terms. God compared Judah to "a green olive tree, beautiful with good fruit" (11:16). But just as lightning can strike a tree down with flames, the Lord would bring destruction on his own people for "making offerings to Baal" (v. 17). They had forsaken God and committed apostasy.

Paul makes use of the analogy of an olive tree to describe the apostasy of Israel in relation to the faith of the Gentiles who have been engrafted into the olive tree. But Paul's language also reveals that amid some of these newly engrafted Gentiles were some who may have been guilty of spiritual pride. Hence, he says, "do not be arrogant toward the branches" (Rom. 11:18). The unbelieving Jews were "broken off because of their unbelief" (v. 20), and the Gentiles were made partakers of the covenant promises through faith. Thus, Paul reminds them again: "do not become proud, but fear" (v. 20). Why? Because if God can judge the natural branches, he can also judge the unnatural branches (v. 21).

There are two contrasting attitudes of God toward two groups of people: severity to those who have fallen in unbelief and pride, and kindness to those who in humble faith continue in or return to his kindness (Rom. 11:22–23). If the Gentiles, or anyone in the visible church today, do not continue in God's kindness, they will also be cut off in their unbelieving drift from the Lord that leads to apostasy (v. 22). Paul highlights that spiritual pride extinguishes faith. You cannot live by faith and be proud of your own spirituality. The life of faith is living in and from the kindness of God, which will always result in humility.

We cannot overstate how much God hates pride. Why else would Paul utter such severe warnings to his Gentile hearers? Consider:

> The fear of the LORD is hatred of evil.
> Pride and arrogance and the way of evil
>   and perverted speech I hate. (Prov. 8:13)

The guilt of Sodom included pride (Ezek. 16:49–50). Thus, "the LORD rained on Sodom and Gomorrah sulfur and fire from the LORD out of heaven" (Gen. 19:24). Sexual perversions, lack of hospitality, and other sins were the result of pride. God's judgment followed, not just with Sodom but also, for example, with King Nebuchadnezzar (Dan. 4:28–33), Miriam (Num. 12), King Uzziah (2 Chron. 26:16), and Herod (Acts 12:21–23).

The Scriptures offer us a harsh reality check concerning pride and the usual consequences: "Pride goes before destruction, and a haughty spirit before a fall" (Prov. 16:18). The fall was brought on by man's pride, which resulted in God's judgment whereby Adam and Eve were excommunicated from Eden. Subsequently, pride has been judged in often severe ways, as Paul shows in Romans 11. But what does pride look like in the backslider and apostate?

The Face of Pride

The manifestation of pride among the people of God begins when the heart says, "My will be done" instead of "Your will be done." As soon as that inclination is allowed to take root and flower, a host of problems arise that pull one away from walking with and living for God.

The sin of pride affects all of Adam's natural descendants, but even the people of God cannot escape the effects of remaining sin that causes pride to rear its ugly head more often than we care to admit. Paul has to remind Christians to live harmoniously with one another and then exhorts them: "Do not be haughty, but associate with the lowly. Never be wise in your own sight" (Rom. 12:16). If one begins to think high things of oneself (v. 3), that person will begin to live in a way that negatively affects the body of Christ. Often disunity happens or a failure to show love when one thinks that he or she is above others. On the contrary, Christians should seek to accommodate themselves to humble people and humble ways. Failing to do this is failing to live according to God's wisdom, since Jesus was "gentle and lowly" (Matt. 11:29). In a certain sense, anyone whom Christ associated with was necessarily far below him in dignity. If the Lord of glory can associate with the humble, then who are we to think that other brothers and sisters are beneath us?

Spiritual pride attacks God as well as the doctrines of justification and sanctification. Regarding the former, every sin is an attack on God—a deicide. Pride causes people to hate God as supreme Ruler: "But Pharaoh said, 'Who is the LORD, that I should obey his voice and let Israel go? I do not know the LORD, and moreover, I will not let Israel go'" (Ex. 5:2). But not just the Pharaohs of the world—when we willfully sin, we are setting ourselves up as Pharaoh: "who is the LORD, that I should obey his [law]?" We elect Satan, not God, to be our lord when we decide to sin against God. When we transgress against God, we are turning against his wisdom and replacing it with our own, thinking that we will receive better blessing and success. But this is stupidity, born from a heart of pride. As we read in Jeremiah:

For my people are foolish;
　　they know me not;
they are stupid children;
　　they have no understanding.
They are "wise"—in doing evil!
　　But how to do good they know not. (Jer. 4:22)

When we exchange the wisdom of God for our own, insisting on our ways over God's ways, we become fools (Rom. 1:22). Besides causing us to hate God's wisdom, pride can also cause us to hate God's mercy. Whether Jonah or the elder brother, we can insist on one standard for ourselves and another standard for others. When we lack knowledge of and appreciation for God's attributes, we can put ourselves in a place where we do not know how to do good (Jer. 4:22). And this will invariably lead to backsliding and sometimes apostasy.

Pride also leads to assaults on our justification and sanctification. Proud people are masters at self-justification. On the one hand, they claim to love the doctrine of justification by faith alone. But the reality of that doctrine means that we must have a sober-minded view of ourselves and admit, more frequently than we do, that we are in the wrong. Sanctification also suffers when pride is not mortified. We can think that we are more holy than we are. Or we do not think we need the means of grace as much as we do, that we will be fine if we give up certain regular habits of worship or prayer. Or we are easily offended because we take ourselves far too seriously. Sanctification certainly leads to Christlikeness, but sanctification should also enable us to have a realistic view of ourselves, namely, that anything good in us is from above.

Pride also lies behind false teaching. And if backsliding happens in a church, it can be the result of unfaithful teaching. These false teachers are, according to Paul, "puffed up with conceit" (1 Tim. 6:4). They possess "an unhealthy craving for controversy and for quarrels about words, which produce envy, dissension, slander, evil suspicions, and constant friction among people who are depraved in mind and deprived of the truth, imagining that godliness is a means of gain" (vv. 4–5). So false teachers are usually unteachable, conjuring up new ideas and doctrines for one reason or another, and these errors have the effect of leading people away from the truth of God's Word. Often when they are publicly corrected, false teachers double down, and their errors become worse over time. Their teaching and their lives are at odds with God's standard for those in authority, and instead of sinking alone, they bring down other souls with them.

Application

As we persevere in the Christian life, we cannot think that pride will have no consequences. There are warnings for those who are proud in their presumption: "Therefore let anyone who thinks that he stands take heed lest he fall" (1 Cor. 10:12). The glorious doctrine of the perseverance of the saints was never understood to allow for a spiritual laziness and presumption.

The warnings or threats that we see in the Scriptures are not hollow, but they must be carefully distinguished based on their intention. John Owen distinguished the different types of threats to unbelievers, false or spurious believers, and true believers. Unbelievers will face judgment for their wickedness and failure to believe in Christ (e.g., John 3:36; Rom. 2:8–9; 2 Thess. 1:6–10; 1 Peter 4:17–18). There are also those who will be judged severely because they were part of the people of God by covenant membership (e.g., Heb. 12:15–17). We might think that the warnings end with these two groups, but warnings are also made to those who are apparently assumed to be true believers (e.g., 1 Cor. 10:12; Heb. 2:3). In connection with this group, Owen claims that these gospel threats toward believers are "suited unto their good and advantage.

... For believers are subject to sloth and security, to wax dead, dull, cold, and formal in their course. . . . To awake them, warn them, and excite them unto a renewal of their obedience, does God set before them the threatenings mentioned. See Rev. 2–3."[7]

Perhaps as you read this, you may be thinking, "Amen, that is so true," without applying it to yourself while thinking, "I'm glad that I don't need to be warned." Is that not a manifestation of the very pride that threatens your soul? Are you wiser than God? Sinclair Ferguson speaks wisely to this issue: "There is no blanket guarantee of perseverance. There is no mere doctrine of the 'security' of the believer, as though God's keeping of us took place irrespective of the lives we live. Indeed there is no such thing in the New Testament as a believer whose perseverance is so guaranteed that he can afford to ignore the warning notes which are sounded so frequently."[8] Those who allow pride to take root in their lives will find that God does not like competition, especially from professing Christians, who should be the most humble of all given the nature of salvation.

There is a salient warning to us in the example of the godly and blessed Hezekiah (see, e.g., 2 Kings 19:14–35), king of Judah, who also holds out hope to us. He was someone who failed to handle the blessings and success of his godly life with care. He became ill to the point of death, but he prayed to the Lord. God mercifully responded with healing (see 2 Kings 20:1–11; Isa. 38:1–22), yet it seems that Hezekiah not only recognized his "faithfulness" but had too high a view of it in connection with his healing. He did not clearly see that his healing ultimately came for the Lord's sake, not because of his supposed worthiness (2 Kings 20:6). Upon his healing, Hezekiah put his own glory on display instead of the Lord's by showing off his wealth to the Babylonian envoys

7. John Owen, *The Works of John Owen*, ed. W. H. Goold, 24 vols. (Edinburgh: T&T Clark, 1850–53), 21:209.

8. Sinclair Ferguson, *The Christian Life: A Doctrinal Introduction* (Edinburgh: Banner of Truth, 1981), 174.

(v. 13), little realizing that this was an invitation for them to one day plunder those riches. In connection with this, Hezekiah's pride was on display because he did not respond to God's merciful healing in humility: "Hezekiah did not make return according to the benefit done to him, for his heart was proud" (2 Chron. 32:25). His heart was lifted up against God. Just as the illness brought Hezekiah to pray, so the judgment of God was used to humble Hezekiah (v. 26). We should take warning here that we avoid like the plague the mentality that we deserve the blessings of the Lord in our lives (see Deut. 9:4–6).

Consider what we noted earlier concerning the fact that we cannot live by faith and be proud of our spirituality. Within the context of the church, we must see how Satan and our flesh can use people's godliness against them. Spiritually minded people excelling in godliness are typically and rightly recognized for their qualities. As DeYoung comments on the thinking of Thomas Aquinas related to the attention that comes for virtue and sanctity: "The better you become, the more recognition typically comes your way; and the more recognition that comes your way, the more susceptible you can become to expecting it and becoming excessively attached to it—to wanting your goodness to be recognized, noticed, affirmed."[9]

God loves us enough to root out pride; he humbles us. Thomas Watson has an interesting comment on the "value" of sin in the life of the Christian: "When a godly man beholds his face in the glass of Scripture, and sees the spots of infidelity and hypocrisy, this makes the plumes of pride fall; they are humbling spots. It is a good use that may be made even of our sins, when they occasion low thoughts of ourselves: better is that sin which humbles me, than that duty which makes me proud."[10]

9. Rebecca Konyndyk DeYoung, *Vainglory: The Forgotten Vice* (Grand Rapids: Eerdmans, 2014), 31.

10. Thomas Watson, *A Divine Cordial: Or, the Transcendent Priviledge of Those That Love God* (London, 1831), 51.

Many times we are humbled by God's fatherly castigations. We can distinguish between his "vindictive punishments" and his "paternal castigations," which, says John Flavel, are the "pure issues of the care and love of a displeased Father."[11] We learn humility through discipline. Hezekiah and the people of Jerusalem experienced God's discipline, and they humbled themselves under his mighty hand (see 1 Peter 5:6). God loves humility so much that he makes wondrous promises to the humble: "Whoever exalts himself will be humbled, and whoever humbles himself will be exalted" (Matt. 23:12).

Finally, we can rid ourselves of pride, hubris, haughtiness, self-exaltation, and the like by carefully meditating on the words of Philippians 2:5–11. The Son willingly humbled himself according to God's will for his life. This meant not just death, but death on a cross. According to Christ's own words, whoever humbles himself will be exalted: Jesus is given the name above every name. He is rewarded, but he was glorified after having been humiliated. A necessary humiliation occurs in the Christian life when we accept that we are sinners who cannot be justified by our works. But even as redeemed saints, we should never forget our free justification; we should remember that we live in God's kindness, and we should accept that sometimes we will suffer to keep us from pride and close to God.

For Further Reflection

1. Why is humility so hard, and how can we better cultivate it in our lives and the lives of others?
2. From the Pharisee and the tax collector in Luke 18:9–14, consider the surprise that the original hearer would have

---

11. John Flavel, *The Works of the Rev. Mr. John Flavel*, 6 vols. (1820; repr., Edinburgh: Banner of Truth, 1997), 3:575.

had about "this man." How does this expose our own pride that is not so easily discerned in the church?

3. Think of a time when you were easily offended. How does this manifest idolatry, and why is it so dangerous?

4. Assuming that it is good to recognize godliness in our own lives and the lives of others, how should we take care about giving such attention?

5. Read and meditate on Isaiah 38:1–22; Jeremiah 11; Luke 18:9–14; Romans 11.

7

The Abandonment of Godly Fear

Therefore, always as a man grows in grace, he grows in awfulness.
... Therefore let us preserve by all means this awful affection, the
fear of God. (Richard Sibbes)[1]

Soul of Godliness

The fear of God is a beautiful but often misunderstood doctrine. Being misunderstood, it gets little attention, with few Christians regarded as, still less honored by being called, God-fearing believers (see Neh. 7:2). In addition, the lack of a healthy fear of God is a universal symptom of backsliding.

When we properly understand this doctrine and make good use of it in our Christian walk, we can bring "holiness to completion in the fear of God" (2 Cor. 7:1). Indeed, it is that very fear of God that draws us and keeps us close to him. John Murray carefully and contextually distinguishes the types of fear in relation to God: "The fear of God which is the soul of godliness does not consist

1. Richard Sibbes, *The Complete Works of Richard Sibbes, D.D.*, 7 vols. (Edinburgh: James Nichol, 1863), 2:53.

... in the dread which is produced by the apprehension of God's wrath. When the reason for such dread exists, then to be destitute of it is the sign of hardened ungodliness."[2]

Speaking of godly fear, which goes beyond a mere fear of judgment, Murray wisely states that

> the dread of judgment will never of itself generate within us the love of God or hatred of the sin that makes us liable to his wrath. Even the infliction of wrath will not create the hatred of sin; it will incite to greater love of sin and enmity against God. Punishment has of itself no regenerating or converting power. The fear of God in which godliness consists is the fear which constrains adoration and love. It is the fear which consists in awe, reverence, honour, and worship, and all of these on the highest level of exercise. It is the reflex in our consciousness of the transcendent majesty and holiness of God. It belongs to all created rational beings and does not take its origins from sin.[3]

If we do not know God and have not meditated on his attributes as revealed in the Scriptures, particularly in books such as the Psalms, Isaiah, and Job, then we will likely have a somewhat anemic fear of God. We do not revere God because we do not know him as we ought. To know him truly is to fear him.

In our analysis of backsliding and apostasy, it is vital not only to highlight the importance of the fear of God in Christian living, but also to distinguish between the reverential fear that all Christians ought to cultivate and the fear of punishment that some professing Christians need to heed when they have reason for such fear.

2. John Murray, *Principles of Conduct: Aspects of Biblical Conduct* (Grand Rapids: Eerdmans, 1971), 236–37.
3. Murray, 237.

Reverential Fear

The fear that all Christians ought to embrace and promote among their fellow brethren is the reverential fear that results from the goal of eternal life: to know the only true God and Jesus Christ (John 17:3). Theologians in the past called this a *filial fear* as opposed to a *servile fear*. Filial fear is a Spirit-wrought grace put into the heart from above in order that we may stay close to our Father in heaven. This type of fear, according to Thomas Manton, consists in a "high esteem of God, of his majesty, glory, power, and in the sense and continual thoughts of his presence. And then a loathness to sin against God, or to offend in his sight, to do anything that is unseemly when God is a looker-on."[4] Our view of God will affect how we act in his presence. If we have low thoughts of him, we will have low thoughts of pleasing him.

Jeremiah 32 contains a wonderful promise concerning such fear that God grants to his children. After highlighting what may be the preeminent promise of the Old Testament—"And they shall be my people, and I will be their God" (Jer. 32:38)—God promises to give them a heart that they may fear him forever: "And I will put the fear of me in their hearts, that they may not turn from me" (v. 40). The promise of God concerning the fear he puts into the hearts of his people is explicitly said to be given that they should not backslide or apostatize.

The Spirit given to us is also the same Spirit given to the Messiah:

> And the Spirit of the LORD shall rest upon him,
>> the Spirit of wisdom and understanding,
>> the Spirit of counsel and might,
>> the Spirit of knowledge and the fear of the LORD. (Isa. 11:2)

---

4. Thomas Manton, *The Complete Works of Thomas Manton*, 22 vols. (London: James Nisbet & Co., 1872), 1:379.

Our Lord possessed a reverential fear of God. He did not shrink back in his obedience because, as one filled with the Spirit, he feared God. As a man, Jesus prayed; he prayed "with loud cries and tears" to God and "was heard because of his reverence" (Heb. 5:7). Knowing the perfections of God, and having such intimate communion with him, Jesus could not but have a reverential fear of God. The horror of his crucifixion was so precisely because he feared God. He knew what justice and holiness looked like and suffered its strokes.

The Spirit in Christ also works fear in us. With a note of hope, Stephen Charnock writes: "And as the Spirit performed his office fully upon the human nature of Christ, so it will not be deficient in us according to our measure. Consider the Spirit every way, and this work of preserving grace will appear to be his business. What Christ doth by his proxy may well be interpreted to be his own act."[5] Christ, personally knowing the value of reverential fear, grants to us that grace that he possesses according to his human nature.

We can trace the value of reverential fear throughout the Scriptures by asking how this illuminates our own view of Christ. For example, why did Jesus have such perfect knowledge? Because the "fear of the LORD is the beginning of knowledge" (Prov. 1:7). If the whole duty of man, according to Solomon, is to "fear God and keep his commandments" (Eccl. 12:13), we can better appreciate why Jesus was able to always do the things pleasing to his Father (John 8:29). Speaking of the sin of presuming upon God's grace, Thomas Watson advises, "Take heed of Presuming: Fear begets Prayer, Prayer begets Strength, and Strength begets Steadfastness."[6] Fear, then, has an infallible connection to our perseverance in the faith.

5. Stephen Charnock, *The Complete Works of Stephen Charnock*, 5 vols. (Edinburgh: James Nichol, 1864–66; repr., Edinburgh: Banner of Truth, 1985), 5:252.

6. Thomas Watson, *A Body of Practical Divinity* (London: Thomas Parkhurst, 1692), 223.

For Christians, in need of redemption through Christ, we can see how our reverential fear is often commanded precisely because of the glorious nature of our salvation. Mary praised God that "his mercy is for those who fear him" (Luke 1:50), and Paul commands the Philippians to "work out your own salvation with fear and trembling" (Phil. 2:12). Salvation is not just something accomplished for us, but the reality of God with us; we live in his presence, which, in the Old Testament, brought about fear because of the greatness of God's redemptive acts (Ex. 15:16). Faith seeking understanding of the attributes of the triune God will beget fear of his great and awesome name.

The positive references to the healthy fear of God are staggering, which makes one wonder why in today's church we seem to have lost this emphasis that is so prominent in God's Word. As children of the Father, living in a world where we are pilgrims and strangers, we should, according to Peter, conduct ourselves with fear (1 Peter 1:17). We should aim to be described by God as Job was: "Have you considered my servant Job, that there is none like him on the earth, a blameless and upright man, who fears God and turns away from evil?" (Job 1:8). This was the glory of the New Testament church: "So the church throughout all Judea and Galilee and Samaria had peace and was being built up. And walking in the fear of the Lord and in the comfort of the Holy Spirit, it multiplied" (Acts 9:31).

Clearly, just as lack of the fear of God leads to sinful conduct (Gen. 20:10–11), so the fear of God is a means to righteous conduct: "Bondservants, obey in everything those who are your earthly masters, not by way of eye-service, as people-pleasers, but with sincerity of heart, fearing the Lord" (Col. 3:22). The fear of God among Christian bondservants in this context is the ground for why their masters can expect sincere obedience. We live under God's watchful omnipresence. We can escape the eyes of man from time to time and shirk various responsibilities, but we can never escape God's eyes. In vain, fallen Adam and Eve hid from God, and his question "Where are you?" (Gen. 3:9) was not because he could not find Adam, but because Adam needed to expose himself before his holy God. And Adam's fear after he sinned was certainly warranted: "And he said, 'I heard the sound of you in the garden, and I was afraid, because I was naked, and I hid myself'" (v. 10). If he were to casually strut around the garden after having so egregiously sinned, it would add to his condemnation. He had reason to fear God's judgment after having sinned.

Coming back to the reality that our ways are before his eyes (Prov. 5:21), we must see not just the all-piercing but also all-protecting eye of God, even as the psalmist exclaims, "Behold, the eye of the LORD is on those who fear him, on those who hope in his steadfast love" (Ps. 33:18). Consider as well David, who identifies the Lord as the all-seeing searcher of thoughts, words, and ways and rhetorically asks: "Where shall I go from your Spirit? Or where shall I flee from your presence?" (139:7). Let us proclaim aloud when we read this, "Nowhere!" Wherever we go, God is. The context indicates that his gaze remains whether we vainly run from God or wonderfully rest under his care and leading, ever held by his "right hand" (v. 10) as a loving Father. As A. A. Anderson notes, the psalmist here "seems to be glad that there is no place in this world" where he is not under the Lord's care while recognizing that "he would have been absolutely foolish to rebel against God, or to try to hide his guilt, had he committed some offense. Therefore, he feels safe with God, and is not afraid to ask God to search his thoughts and motives."[7] Clearly, there exists a sense of both awe and adoration in the fear of God, both essential elements of worship and bound together without tension. Indeed, as James Houston observes, "Fear, or reverence for God," involves "both distance as

---

7. A. A. Anderson, *The Book of Psalms*, vol. 2, *Psalms 73–150*, New Century Bible Commentary (Grand Rapids: Eerdmans, 1992), 907.

awe, even a holy terror, and ... proximity and communion."[8] For example, Psalm 2:11 testifies of our service in "fear" of the Lord, whose blessed refuge and deliverance give us cause to "rejoice" in him while taking him seriously and tempered with "trembling."

Thus, there exists a glorious irony in the reverential fear of God, in that it so powerfully indicates his intimacy with those who express it, truly a manifestation of filial fear. Those who take our Father the most seriously are those who run to him most quickly and experience his love most powerfully. In light of this, consider such passages as these: "The friendship of the LORD is for those who fear him" (Ps. 25:14); "those who fear him have no lack" (34:9); "the LORD shows compassion to those who fear him" (103:13); "the steadfast love of the LORD is from everlasting to everlasting on those who fear him" (103:17; see also 5:7); "his salvation is near to those who fear him" (85:9; see also Isa. 33:6; Acts 13:26); and "the LORD takes pleasure in those who fear him, in those who hope in his steadfast love" (Ps. 147:11).

There are times when a threat is made in God's Word to professing Christians to help them, not harm them. We could simply eradicate in our preaching and teaching any form of warning because it might cause a servile fear. But good theologians have not been swayed by such sophistry. Speaking of the value of divine threats, Octavius Winslow argues that when such warnings are received in the heart as from a holy God, the effect will be holiness.[9] John Owen rejects the idea that divine threats lead to servile fear. This is a "vain" imagination, since only the "bondage of our own spirits may make every thing we do servile."[10] In fact, far from

8. James M. Houston, *I Believe in the Creator* (Grand Rapids: Eerdmans, 1980), 188.

9. Octavius Winslow, *Personal Declension and Revival of Religion in the Soul* (Eugene, OR: Wipf and Stock, 2001), 147.

10. John Owen, *The Works of John Owen*, ed. W. H. Goold, 24 vols. (Edinburgh: T&T Clark, 1850–53), 3:614.

causing bondage, God's threats and promises are a "principal part of our liberty."[11]

When God speaks of his wrath on unrepentant sinners, we should, as those who believe God's Word, be deterred from living as "the sons of disobedience" (Eph. 5:6; see also Col. 3:5–6). Manton calls God's promise of judgment to the impenitent not only a "powerful motive" but also a "kindly motive."[12] He offers several reasons why God's threat of punishment is an act of kindness. Since sin is displeasing to God, we need to see both its evil and its effects so that we can appreciate God's justice in punishing sin. To not take seriously God's punishment of sin is to not take God himself seriously. In Ezekiel's time, the house of Israel accused God of not being just when in fact it was the Israelites who lacked justice. They were commanded to repent or be judged, though God claims to take no pleasure in such judgment (Ezek. 18:30–32). In addition, for those who love God, the thought of being without him is awful. Manton notes, "A man cannot love God and not fear the loss of his favour."[13] The fear of God's punishment toward those who willfully engage in sin helps us to do what is right: "As one nail drives out another," says Manton, "so the fear of God drives out the fear of men and pleasing lusts: Rom. 8:13, 'If you live after the flesh you shall die.'"[14] This leads to an important pastoral observation by Manton:

> The effect which it must produce is not such a fear as drives us from God, but brings us to him; not torment, and perplexity, and despairing anguish . . . , but flight and caution. We ought to represent it as a great evil, from when we must fly by faith and repentance . . . to quicken us in our flight to Christ, and taking

11. Owen, 3:614.
12. Manton, *Works*, 19:228.
13. Manton, 19:229.
14. Manton, 19:229.

sanctuary at the grace of the gospel; and to engage us to more thankfulness for our deliverance by Christ.[15]

This agrees with Murray above that mere fear of punishment is not enough; it may awaken us, but only by faith and repentance, with the hope of taking sanctuary in Christ, can it bring us back to God.

With the teaching above in mind, we can perhaps understand the language of a warning passage such as Hebrews 10:25–31 both as a legitimate warning (not hypothetical) and as a means used by the author to exhort professing Christians to not give up what is most important, namely, corporate worship where we stir one another up to love and good works. If a professing Christian willfully neglects corporate worship for a sustained period, without any apparent good reason, that person has reason to be afraid of God's judgment accordingly. It would be impious to lack such fear —and it is usually lacking in those who stop worshiping publicly. Hebrews 10:25–31 issues forth severe warnings to deliberate sinners. To such people "there no longer remains a sacrifice for sins, but a fearful expectation of judgment, and a fury of fire that will consume the adversaries" (Heb. 10:26–27). "It is," says the author, "a fearful thing to fall into the hands of the living God" (v. 31). Yet when we live with fear, understood as reverential awe in the presence of God, taking him seriously, we are being protected from having to be counted as those who should have the fear of dread and punishment.

Jerry Bridges rightfully states that God's Word "often links a lack of the fear of God with sinful conduct."[16] Those professing to know Christ without a changed life that results in dying to sin and living for him, those in whom sin does not just remain but reigns as "they go on sinning deliberately" (e.g., abandoning corporate

15. Manton, 19:229.
16. Jerry Bridges, *The Joy of Fearing God* (Colorado Springs: WaterBrook Press, 2009), 21.

worship, Heb. 10:25) in spite of a full knowledge of gospel truth (v. 26), cannot claim that Christ took their judgment for them on the cross, but live under "a fearful expectation of judgment" themselves in hell (v. 27). It is a real warning for all, yet for true believers it is enough that they hear, for example, of the vital importance of attending church and so respond accordingly. Yet those living without the fear of God, and who fail to take him seriously, think nothing of neglecting church and stand (perhaps ignorantly or even indifferently) under "fearful expectation" while living in a way that they profanely trample Christ and the grace of salvation underfoot (v. 29). The warning is meant to awaken them to their sin that they may yet escape damnation by faith (whether renewed or brand-new) for the preservation of their souls (vv. 37–39).

The fear of punishment is held out to professing Christians for various reasons—for example: (1) failure to bear fruit (John 15:1–11); (2) spiritual pride (Rom. 11:11–24); (3) unbelief (Heb. 3–4); (4) spiritual lukewarmness (Rev. 3:14–22); (5) toleration of false teaching (Rev. 2:20–23); (6) living according to the flesh (Rom. 8:13; Gal. 5:21). Either all these warnings are meaningless (or merely hypothetical) or they are offered from a gracious God who does not wish to see any perish, but desires that through faith and repentance we should turn back to him. If he sees fit to warn certain people who are engaging in actions that draw them away from living for his glory, then who are we to deny the value of appropriate fear of punishment? Only we must always provide hope for those who are being warned!

Application

One of the most obvious symptoms of backsliding is lacking the reverential fear of God that keeps us in close communion with him and his people. When we fail to take him seriously, abandoned, we find that another fear comes to the foreground: the lasting fear of punishment. Sadly, many who lack reverential fear are not moved by warnings. But we must still warn those who need to be warned, just as we must comfort those who need to be comforted. There is a time for everything under the sun, and one of the difficulties of being a faithful pastor or Christian friend is knowing when to warn and when to comfort, when to rebuke and when to encourage.

How about you? Do you see yourself as someone who needs to be warned at times? Most Christians will affirm that they do—until the warning actually comes and they quickly take offense and dig in their heels of vehement denial and self-defense. But when we consider that the Lord shows mercy to those who freely confess their sins (1 John 1:9), why not be silent, patiently listen to the warning, and prayerfully reflect on it? Ask the Lord to search your heart that your sinful thoughts, words, and actions might be dealt with in Christ's grace of forgiveness and transformation. Be thankful that the Lord uses others to help you be watchful in the Christian life in the fear of the Lord. Besides, as John Bunyan reflects: "This grace of fear . . . is that tender, sensible, and trembling grace that keeps the soul upon its continual watch. To keep a good watch is, you know, a wonderful safety to a place that is in continual danger because of the enemy."[17]

Another fear that arises in the hearts of those who do not fear God is the fear of man. Jesus places us in one of two categories when he exhorts: "And do not fear those who kill the body but cannot kill the soul. Rather fear him who can destroy both soul and body in hell" (Matt. 10:28). Remember, the one whom you fear is the one whose favor you seek. You may have noticed this earlier in the mention of Colossians 3:22 in the context of our conduct under the fear of God. But notice also that in this passage, we live either as "people-pleasers" in fear of men or as God-pleasers, "fearing" him. Ask yourself the following when you are fearful in speaking

---

17. John Bunyan, *The Fear of God* (London: Religious Tract Society, 1839), 166.

for Christ, a struggle that we all have: "The LORD is my light and my salvation; whom shall I fear? The LORD is the stronghold of my life; of whom shall I be afraid?" (Ps. 27:1). We can be guilty of what has been called *toxic empathy*. A brother or sister in Christ is clearly not living in the fear of God, but we fail to speak honestly to that person because we don't want him or her to dislike us.

We must also remember that one of the signs of a godless person is a lack of fear of God: "There is no fear of God before their eyes" (Rom. 3:18). In his commentary on this verse, Murray explains the importance of connecting the lack of the fear of God with the eyes:

> The eyes are the organs of vision and the fear of God is appropriately expressed as before our eyes because the fear of God means that God is constantly in the center of our thought and apprehension, and life is characterized by the all-pervasive consciousness of dependence upon him and responsibility to him. The absence of this fear means that God is excluded not only from the centre of thought and calculation but from the whole horizon of our reckoning; God is not in all our thoughts. Figuratively, he is not before our eyes. And this is unqualified godlessness.[18]

Do you see God by faith daily, longing to see him by sight in the face of Jesus Christ? That is godliness.

We are to be like Job, "who feared God and turned away from evil" (Job 1:1). And as we live in the presence of God, sometimes going through many trials, but seeing him faithfully, wisely, graciously, and mercifully bringing us through those trials, we can also say with Job:

> I had heard of you by the hearing of the ear,
>   but now my eye sees you. (Job 42:5)

---

18. John Murray, *The Epistle to the Romans* (Grand Rapids: Eerdmans, 1997), 105.

We can live with the reverential fear of God before our eyes, knowing that "the LORD takes pleasure in those who fear him, in those who hope in his steadfast love" (Ps. 147:11). The thought that our fear of God is connected to the pleasure he takes in us is another reason why we should not be ashamed to teach and promote the fear of the Lord. In sum, to the degree that we grow in the fear of the Lord, we will grow in Christlikeness, for no one ever marveled at the excellencies of God more than the one who was face to face with God (John 1:1, 18).

For Further Reflection

1. How has the fear of God affected your Christian walk?
2. Why is it so important that we consciously pursue a filial fear of God in the Christian life rather than a servile fear?
3. Name some situations in which people-pleasing tendencies lead us to fear man rather than God. How can we address such tendencies?
4. Read and meditate on Jeremiah 32:36–44; John 15:1–11; Revelation 2:18–29.

8

The Death of Mortification

God's promises to us are more powerful and effectual for the mortifying of sin than our promises to God. (Matthew Henry)[1]

Who Is Killing?

While the healthy Christian seeks ardently to kill sin, the backslider has stopped waging war against the flesh by the Spirit. Only those who have been given new life from above, have received the Spirit, have been justified freely by his grace, and live as children of God can expect to have any success against remaining indwelling sin. Only such people strive to put sin to death. But sometimes such desires wane, and we stop fighting the good fight and slowly exchange the armor of God for a bathing suit in which we lounge with sin as though relaxing at the beach.

"For if you live according to the flesh you will die," Romans 8:13 tells us, "but if by the Spirit you put to death the deeds of the body, you will live." This has proved to be a justly well-known text

---

1. Matthew Henry, *An Exposition of the Several Epistles Contained in the New Testament* [...] (London: John Clark, 1721), 24.

concerning the duty of all believers as they progress in holiness. It is not hard to understand the text, but obeying its command might be the most difficult duty that Christians face. The mortification (putting to death) of sin occupies a central place in Christian treatments on sanctification.

In this text, there exists a threat, based on a condition: "For if you live according to the flesh you will die." There is also a promise: "you will live." The promise is based on the successful performance of a duty: "if by the Spirit you put to death the deeds of the body." The agents include the Christian and the Spirit: "if by the Spirit you." The "you" refers to those who are no longer under condemnation (Rom. 8:1) and possess the Spirit of Christ (v. 9).

At this point we might worry that the condition will not be met by true Christians. Some immaturely ask, when told that good works are necessary for a Christian, "How many good works are needed?" I wonder whether they would also say, "How much mortification is needed in order to live?" Before answering that question, we can understand this condition ("if") as one whereby, to use John Owen's words, there is a "certainty of coherence."[2] By this he expresses that specific means will definitely bring a particular end. As part of the gift of salvation, true believers will receive many blessings, including justification, adoption, sanctification, and glorification. The goal of our salvation is conformity, in body and soul, to Jesus Christ: "But our citizenship is in heaven, and from it we await a Savior, the Lord Jesus Christ, who will transform our lowly body to be like his glorious body, by the power that enables him even to subject all things to himself" (Phil. 3:20–21).

The means to the end (glorification) includes putting to death the old man in each born-again Christian. Only the justified person can be sanctified, but only the sanctified person will be

2. John Owen, *The Works of John Owen*, ed. W. H. Goold, 24 vols. (Edinburgh: T&T Clark, 1850–53), 6:6.

glorified. Sanctification is, according to Thomas Watson, "Heaven begun in the Soul. Sanctification and Glory differ only in degree; Sanctification is Glory in the Seed, and Glory is Sanctification in the Flower."[3] They have an infallible connection. Thus, Owen says that the conditional language of Paul in Romans 8:13 should be understood in terms of a "certain infallible connection and coherence between true mortification and eternal life: if you use this means, you shall obtain that end; if you do mortify, you shall live."[4] While we do not wish to rob the conditional "if" of its true force, we have to understand this verse in light of all that Paul has said in the book of Romans, which gives us confidence that we will meet the condition because of God's faithfulness to his promise.

The Daily Duty

We are by nature lovers of pleasure and not pain. Even for Christians, this principle remains. It is not necessarily bad, for we ought to long for true "pleasures forevermore" (Ps. 16:11). But sin latches on to the wrong pleasures (e.g., looking at pornography) or turns good pleasures (e.g., eating) into wrong pleasures (e.g., gluttony). Killing sinful desires is not easy or fun, but it is necessary (Col. 3:1–10).

Christians, living in the Spirit, are able to not sin. When they mortify sin, they strike at the root of sin in the hope that the branches that flow from it wither. Thomas Goodwin claims that all our sinful desires are rooted in the "love of pleasure more than of God" (see 2 Tim. 3:4).[5] Goodwin adds that mortification deadens us to sin's pleasure "by bringing the heart more into communion

---

3. Thomas Watson, *A Body of Practical Divinity* [...] (London: Thomas Parkhurst, 1692), 216.

4. Owen, *Works*, 6:6.

5. Thomas Goodwin, *The Works of Thomas Goodwin*, 12 vols. (Edinburgh: James Nichol, 1861–66; repr., Grand Rapids: Reformation Heritage Books, 2006), 3:503.

and into love with God."[6] Thus, "the choicest believers," to use Owen's words, "ought to make it their business all their days to mortify the indwelling power of sin" because this brings them into closer communion with the triune God.[7]

Indwelling sin, even though we strike at it and land blows to its root, never ever rests in this life. Sin keeps us from the good and inclines us toward that which is evil. "Sin is," says Owen, "always acting, always conceiving, always seducing and tempting. . . . There is not a day but sin foils or is foiled, prevails or is prevailed on; and it will be so whilst we live in this world."[8] Because sin is a busy thing, full of vigor, if we give up mortification "it will *bring forth great, cursed, scandalous, soul-destroying sins.*"[9] Thus, the person who fails to mortify sin will inevitably backslide and, if the practice is omitted altogether, will apostatize.

Failure to mortify sin opposes the purposes of sanctification. Owen vividly argues that "negligence in this duty casts the soul into a perfect contrary condition to that which the apostle affirms was his."[10] Paul states, "Though our outer self is wasting away, our inner self is being renewed day by day" (2 Cor. 4:16). When backsliders put mortification rather than sin to death, the inward man perishes, with the outer self often becoming the focus of one's daily efforts. Owen adds that "by the omission of this duty grace withers, lust flourishes, and the frame of the heart grows worse and worse; and the Lord knows what desperate and fearful issues it has had with many."[11]

Writing to believers in the church, who were to guard against false teachers, John warns: "Watch yourselves, so that you may not

6. Goodwin, 3:503.
7. Owen, *Works*, 6:7.
8. Owen, 6:11.
9. Owen, 6:12.
10. Owen, 6:13.
11. Owen, 6:13.

lose what we have worked for, but may win a full reward. Everyone who goes on ahead and does not abide in the teaching of Christ, does not have God. Whoever abides in the teaching has both the Father and the Son" (2 John 8–9). Evidently, John had to admonish his hearers to watchfulness so that they would not lose what the apostles had worked so hard for in their ministry to these believers.

Many Christians have spoken of Owen's work on mortification with admiration for his thoroughness, precision, and incisiveness. But he admonishes the "professors" of his day who, "instead of bringing forth such great and evident fruits of mortification as are expected, scarce bear any leaves of it. . . . The good Lord send out a spirit of mortification to cure our distempers, or we are in a sad condition!"[12] It is one thing to cite Owen's work on mortification, but another to actually put sin to death. Yet this must be the aim of all Christians, one more difficult than familiarity with the verse and topic.

I Believe in the Holy Spirit

When we ask our Father to give us more of his Holy Spirit, we may not be aware what that will mean. For example, the fruit of the Spirit in Galatians 5:22–23 includes patience. If we pray for the Spirit to fill us, should we not also expect for God to providentially and lovingly test our patience in situations in which this grace can grow by the Spirit's work? We all want to be filled with the Spirit, but do we want the circumstances that the Lord wisely ordains for it to happen?

The work of the Spirit, then, aims at death (mortification) and life (vivification): death of the old man and the putting on of the new man. We bring forth acts of sin because the habit is still present within us. Similarly, we bring forth acts of faith because

12. Owen, 6:14–15.

we possess the habit of faith implanted by the Spirit. He works to weaken and destroy the habit of sin, though not apart from our own willing. Sanctification is not, for lack of a better term, monergistic, as if God were the only one who works (see Phil. 2:12–13). A synergy is involved that we must insist on, which explains why backsliders are at fault for their negligence.

Owen maintains that while our mortification cannot happen apart from the work of the Spirit, it is "still an act of our obedience." He adds that the Spirit "works in us and upon us, as we are fit to be wrought in and upon; that is, so as to preserve our own liberty and free obedience. He works upon our understandings, wills, consciences, and affections, agreeably to their own natures he works *in us* and *with us*, not *against us* or *without us*; so that his assistance is an encouragement as to the facilitating of the work, and no occasion of neglect as to the work itself."[13] Similarly, Stephen Charnock views mortification as a work whereby man is a willing agent, though manifestly not by his own strength: "We must engage in the duel, but it is the strength of the Spirit only can render us victorious. The duty is ours, but the success is from God. Every believer is *principium activum*, but the Spirit is *principium effectivum*. We can sin of ourselves, but not overcome sin by ourselves; we know how to be slaves, but are unable of ourselves to be conquerors. As God made us first free, so he only can restore us to that freedom we have lost, and does it by his Spirit, which is a Spirit of liberty."[14] We are the "active principle" (agent), but the Spirit is the "effective principle" (agent), foundationally and graciously working holiness in us. The Spirit gives us freedom to obey, power to mortify. The words of Jonathan Edwards quoted in chapter 2 bear repeating, as he says of sanctification: "God is the

---

13. Owen, 6:20.

14. Stephen Charnock, *The Complete Works of Stephen Charnock*, 5 vols. (Edinburgh: James Nichol, 1864–66; repr., Edinburgh: Banner of Truth, 1985), 5:216.

only proper author and fountain; we only are the proper actors. We are in different respects, wholly passive and wholly active."[15]

Speaking of the Spirit as a "voluntary agent," Goodwin makes a provocative point about the Spirit's powerful work in the lives of the sanctified, namely, that those with "more habitual grace shall be more assisted and enlivened" (see Matt. 25:29). Received habits of grace result in acts of obedience, and the more we receive, the more we act. God "delights still to crown his own works in us with more."[16] Simply put, acts of obedience lead to further acts of obedience. Righteousness begets righteousness. The obedient does not quench or grieve the Spirit, but rather increases in fruits of righteousness. As Goodwin argues, "every act of grace does, through the blessing of the Spirit, further sanctify and increase the habit. . . . When they do any duty, it makes the heart more inwardly holy, so as indeed the one cannot be without the other; but the more a man does abstain out of right principles, by the assistance of the Spirit, the more he grows: so as in the end all comes to one; he whose holiness is acted most has in the end most habitual grace."[17] "The more sin dies," observes Charnock, "the more the soul lives."[18] Or, as Owen affirms, "Mortification prunes all the graces of God, and makes room for them in our hearts to grow."[19] The more we kill sin, the more alive to God we will be.

Grieving the Spirit

Backsliders stop waging war against the flesh only to find that they lose the peace of conscience they once enjoyed with God.

15. Jonathan Edwards, *The Works of President Edwards*, 4 vols. (New York: Leavitt & Allen, 1856), 2:580.

16. Goodwin, *Works*, 3:493.

17. Goodwin, 3:493–94.

18. Charnock, *Works*, 5:216.

19. Owen, *Works*, 6:23.

Their loss of peace goes hand in hand with their lack of godly vitality. Our strength comes from the work of the Spirit, but when we fail to actively mortify sin, not only do we lose our sense of enjoyment, peace, and communion with God, but we also grieve the Holy Spirit. The latter occurs as we grant to sin a vigor that it does not deserve. This is a horrendous crime against God, who graciously gives us the Spirit of Christ to make us like Christ. But instead of living a Spirit-filled and Spirit-dependent life, backsliders live the Spirit-grieved life.

The Holy Spirit is not able to be "grieved," properly speaking, as though he had passions, and could suffer or change his disposition toward us because of our actions against him. Indeed, God is without passions, which does not deny his expressions of love or compassion or wrath as outward acts of the will, but denotes an immutable God not subject to change as affected by some external agent. The language used in the Scriptures speaks of God's various passions metaphorically and as gracious condescensions toward us in our weakness in understanding divine things. Octavius Winslow attests that such expressions of "grief" or "anger," for example, "set forth God's extreme hatred of sin, and the holy sensitiveness of the Eternal Spirit to any neglect, undervaluing, of declension of his most gracious work and influence in the soul."[20] The Spirit is a person, and we are to fellowship with him, the one who brings us to the Father through Christ. When we disregard the Spirit and, to use Winslow's words, "oppose his influence, and slight his kind, loving, and tender nature," we can "cause a withdrawment from the soul —in some cases temporary, in others eternal—of his presence, influence and blessings."[21]

---

20. Octavius Winslow, *Personal Declension and Revival of Religion in the Soul* (Eugene, OR: Wipf and Stock, 2001), 191.
   21. Winslow, 191.

As holy people, being sanctified by faith, we are to put off the old man and put on the new man. For example, we "put away falsehood" (Eph. 4:25); we allow "no corrupting talk" to proceed from our lips (v. 29); and we must not "grieve the Holy Spirit of God" (v. 30). Grieving the Spirit has a sad history among the people of God.

God's grace has been spurned by his own ungrateful people from the beginning as they rebel against him. In fact, Isaiah adds that God's people "grieved his Holy Spirit" (Isa. 63:10; see also Ps. 78:40) as a distinct Being who is holy and has been spurned. Such corporate rebellion against the Spirit carries on in the New Testament when Stephen denounces the unbelieving Jews as "stiff-necked people" (Acts 7:51) like the golden-calf-idolater Israelites (Ex. 33:3–5). Stephen goes on to declare that "you always resist the Holy Spirit" (Acts 7:51), manifesting an unwelcome pattern of Spirit opposition among God's people through the history of redemption. Not surprisingly, then, Paul warns the Thessalonians, who are generally blameless in contrast to the Galatians or Corinthians, to not quench the Spirit (1 Thess. 5:19) as if extinguishing a fire. This vivid image expresses the restraint that our sin places on the work of the Spirit in our lives.

In certain respects, then, the sins of those who profess the faith are worse than the sins of those who are pagans. Charnock makes this point with his usual clarity:

> For other men sin against natural, you against spiritual principles; others sin against an habit of common notion, you against an habit of divine grace. A natural man sins against the *light* of God in his conscience, a renewed man against the *life* of God in his heart. Others sin against a Christ crucified and risen from the grave; he sins against a Christ new-formed and risen in his heart. Others sin against the law of God in the word, he against the law written in his mind and word too. Such cast dirt

upon the Spirit's work, cross the end of so noble a piece, bring a thief into the Spirit's temple, and grieve the Holy Spirit, who instructed him better. Whenever you sin, it must cost you more grief, because your sins are more grievous; and you must grieve the more for them, because the Spirit is grieved by them. Grief for sin is a standing grace in the new creature, and part of a likeness to the Spirit of God, whatsoever some men dream to the contrary.[22]

Our spiritual blessings bring with them great responsibilities, so much so that God has higher expectations of those called his children in their expected battle with sin. Given the benefits of salvation that we have received, our sin against the Spirit of sanctification is all the more grievous. Thus, lukewarmness in Christians is abhorrent sin in the eyes of Christ. How can those who have received so much respond with indifference?

God has shown his love for us in the giving not only of his only Son to accomplish our salvation (Rom. 8:32), but also of the Spirit to apply it in our hearts and graciously enable living communion with the triune God. Professing believers should be encouraged to remember that if we dishonor the Spirit when we willfully and habitually engage in sin, we also honor him when we walk in holiness. Pleasing God should have a greater sway upon the children of God than it does. When we grieve the Spirit, we grieve Christ. We are laying blows to him and giving his adversary, the devil, gratification. Christ should be gratified, not the devil. To the extent that we mortify sin by the Spirit, we glorify God and wound the devil. To the degree that we give up mortification and become hardened by sin's deceitfulness, we glorify the devil and wound Christ.

---

22. Charnock, *Works*, 3:136.

Application

Those justified freely by God's grace and having received the Spirit of adoption have no option but to wage war against sin. God chose us to be holy and blameless in his sight (Eph. 1:4), which denotes the call to Christlikeness. God's promises will not fail—we will become like Christ through the work of the Spirit (Rom. 8:9, 29). But the means to accomplish this end include putting to death our sin nature.

Why should we put to death the deeds of the flesh? Because God delights in righteousness and has no pleasure in wickedness. Goodwin, in *The Heart of Christ in Heaven towards Sinners on Earth*, provided one of the most heartwarming books of Christ ever written. It has been a balm to many souls who have felt the weight of their sins and wondered how Christ could love us despite our repeated offenses against him. But we should not miss what Goodwin claims is the greatest motive for killing sin (i.e., mortification) and obeying God (i.e., vivification): "to consider that Christ's heart, if it be not afflicted with—and how far it may suffer with us we know not—yet for certain has less joy in us, as we are more or less sinful, or obedient. You know not by sin what blows you give the heart of Christ. If no more but that his joy is the less in you, it should move you [to obey]."[23] Should not our love for Christ keep us from sinning against him?

This love of complacency stirs us up to holiness, even as we read in John 14:21: "Whoever has my commandments and keeps them, he it is who loves me. And he who loves me will be loved by my Father, and I will love him and manifest myself to him." While we affirm an unconditional love of benevolence (goodwill) toward us from before the foundation of the world, we can also affirm that God delights in his creatures according to the degree of loveliness

23. Goodwin, *Works*, 4:150.

in them.[24] Watson makes the point starkly: "The more we grow in Grace, the more will God love us. Is it not that we pray for? The more Growth, the more will God love us."[25]

We may find this hard to accept, but some Christians are more holy than others. In terms of holiness, we cannot mortify sin without the Spirit, but we are still responsible, according to the habit of grace in us, to perform that very work. Mortification occurs based on a Christian's possession of the habit. The act is ours; the power comes from above. When we fail to mortify, we cannot blame God. Our backsliding is precisely that: *ours*, not his.

Those who do not take mortification seriously trivialize sin. When we drink in sin daily without proper repentance, we presume upon the grace of God. Owen attests that there exists no "greater evidence of a false and rotten heart in the world" than those who live lasciviously.[26] He adds, "To use the blood of Christ, which is given to *cleanse* us, 1 John 1:7, Titus 2:14; the exaltation of Christ, which is to give us *repentance*, Acts 5:31; the doctrine of grace, which teaches us to *deny all ungodliness*, Titus 2:11, 12, to countenance sin, is a rebellion that in the issue will break the bones. At this door have gone out from us most of the professors that have apostatized in the days wherein we live."[27]

We have been delivered from the wrath to come—not merely from God's wrath, but also into friendship with him. Our mortification should result not only from our horror over the evil of sin and its awful effects in our lives (and the lives of others) but also from our desire to have intimate communion with the triune God.

---

24. One could read many excellent treatments of the distinction between God's love of benevolence and complacency, but Charnock's is clear. See *Works*, 3:344–45; 5:222.

25. Watson, *Body of Practical Divinity*, 216.

26. Owen, *Works*, 6:15.

27. Owen, 6:15.

For Further Reflection

1. Is the Christian life better described as active or passive? How does the concept of holy war help us to understand the Christian life?
2. How do Christians sometimes misunderstand the way in which the Spirit works in our lives?
3. Do Christians think about grieving the Spirit? If not, why not?
4. Read and meditate on Romans 8:1–13; Colossians 3:1–17.

9

The Neglect of Prayer

*What is the cause of most backslidings? I believe, as a general rule,
one of the chief causes is neglect of private prayer. You may be very
sure men fall in private long before they fall in public. They are
backsliders on their knees long before they backslide openly in the
eyes of the world.* (J. C. Ryle)[1]

Private and Corporate

Prayer, even for the Christian who is walking with the Lord,
is often difficult. As Martyn Lloyd-Jones well noted, "Everything
we do in the Christian life is easier than prayer."[2] The flesh, devil,
and world are powerful foes that keep many from communion
with God. Thomas Brooks observed, "David's heart was oft more
out of tune than his harp," but prayer was what brought his heart
back into tune with God.[3]

1. J. C. Ryle, *A Call to Prayer* (Carlisle, PA: Banner of Truth, 2002), 16.
2. D. Martyn Lloyd-Jones, *Studies in the Sermon on the Mount* (Nottingham,
England: Inter-Varsity Press, 1976), 362.
3. Thomas Brooks, *Precious Remedies against Satan's Devices* [. . .] (Philadelphia:
Jonathan Pounder, 1810), 316.

In life, we all do the things we really want to do. We have a surprising amount of energy for various activities. Some parents drive across a city to get their child to a sports practice or a music lesson. Some people never miss a day of exercise; others religiously make time for their favorite cable-streamed shows on a weekly, or even daily, basis. So when it comes to the backsliding Christian, we can expect that one of the most difficult spiritual exercises in the Christian life—prayer!—will suffer.

Octavius Winslow argues that if we were to choose a "single characteristic of personal declension more marked than another," it would no doubt be the "decay of the spirit of prayer as that feature."[4] We can take this a step further to claim that this neglect concerns not only private but also public communion and prayer with the triune God.

A person who abandons prayer is like a person who struggles to breathe. Eventually, without sufficient oxygen, the effects are obvious, sometimes fatal. A vigorous prayer life advances the soul to greater dependence on and love for God and soul-enriching communion with him, which should always be our goal. This ought to happen both in private and in public.

When we look at the scriptural evidence, we cannot escape the reality that private and corporate prayer are evidence of spiritual vitality. Jesus assumes that his followers will pray privately: "But when you pray, go into your room and shut the door and pray to your Father who is in secret. And your Father who sees in secret will reward you" (Matt. 6:6). The early Christians were likewise devoted to corporate prayer: "All these with one accord were devoting themselves to prayer, together with the women and Mary the mother of Jesus, and his brothers" (Acts 1:14); "And they devoted themselves to . . . the prayers" (2:42); "When he

---

4. Octavius Winslow, *Personal Declension and Revival of Religion in the Soul* (Eugene, OR: Wipf and Stock, 2001), 112.

realized this, he went to the house of Mary, the mother of John whose other name was Mark, where many were gathered together and were praying" (12:12). In line with the previous chapter, these two aspects of prayer are vital to maintaining a proper fear of God. Approaching him in prayer resists turning away from him. We approach him affectionately as our heavenly Father, the one who lovingly rewards those who seek him (Heb. 11:6).

Our communion with God, often in prayer, is something to be maintained to withstand the devil. As Brooks affirms, "a soul high in communion with God may be tempted, but will not easily be conquered, such a soul will fight it out to the death."[5]

The Difficulty of Prayer

The answer to the question why backsliders neglect prayer is partially found in understanding the benefits of prayer, but even with such benefits at hand we still struggle because of our remaining weakness even in a state of grace.

Theologians from the early church have spoken of prayer as conversation with God whereby we contemplate invisible realities. As children of God, we think of prayer as familiar conversation with our Father in heaven. Winslow wonderfully calls it "communion of the spiritual life in the soul of man with its Divine Author; it is a breathing back the Divine life into the bosom of God from whence it came; it is holy, spiritual, humble converse with God."[6] When we experience these realities daily, we draw near to the living God, since we are breathing back his life to him, knowing that we will receive it afresh from him.

Stephen Charnock attests that prayer is a "general means for everything we want, but ought to be more pressed than any, both

---

5. Brooks, *Precious Remedies against Satan's Devices*, 314.
6. Winslow, *Personal Declension*, 112–13.

because of its universal influence, and the common deplorable neglect or slight performance of it."[7] In other words, we must see the importance of prayer not only because of its power but also because our weakness to pray gives rise to "the common deplorable neglect . . . of it." Indeed, as John Bunyan testifies:

> May I but speak my own experience, and from that tell you the difficulty of praying to God as I ought; it is enough to make you poor, blind, carnal men, to entertain strange thoughts of me. For, as for my heart, when I go to pray, I find it so reluctant to go to God, and when it is with him, so reluctant to stay with him, that many times I am forced in my prayers; first to beg God that he would take mine heart, and set it on himself in Christ, and when it is there, that he would keep it there. In fact, many times I know not what to pray for, I am so blind, nor how to pray I am so ignorant; only (blessed be Grace) the *Spirit helps our infirmities* [Rom. 8:26].[8]

Bunyan opens his heart as a typical believer struggling to pray and wanting to do better. In line with this reluctance, Alexander Whyte observes: "There is nothing in which we need to take so many lessons as in prayer . . . ; there is nothing in which we are so helpless. And there is nothing else that we are so bad at all our days. We have an inborn, a constitutional, a habitual, and, indeed, an hereditary dislike of prayer."[9] Many more testimonies could be offered by theologians, pastors, and Christians throughout

---

7. Stephen Charnock, *The Complete Works of Stephen Charnock*, 5 vols. (Edinburgh: James Nichol, 1864–66; repr., Edinburgh: Banner of Truth, 1985), 4:101.

8. John Bunyan, *The Works of That Eminent Servant of Christ, John Bunyan* [. . .], 3 vols. (New Haven, CT: Nathan Whiting, 1830), 2:547.

9. Alexander Whyte, *Lord, Teach Us to Pray: Sermons on Prayer* (Vancouver: Regent College Publishing, 1998), 257.

the ages concerning the difficulty of prayer. All true believers can identify with this challenge.

We open our Bibles and God speaks to us, but when we "close" our Bibles we ought to speak to God.[10] Indeed, those open pages testify of the need for and the blessing of fervent prayer. Christian believers need constant reminders, encouragements, and exhortations to pray from the Word as read, proclaimed, and shared by and with the Spirit. We are not naturally prone to converse with the God we cannot physically see. Yet in Christ, possessing the Spirit of Christ in our souls, we will cry out to God even as the Spirit has taught us (Gal. 4:6). Not surprisingly, one mark of a backslider is the neglect of prayer. Consequently, we must ardently own and confront our tendency to "prayersliding."

Cures for Prayersliding

There does not appear to be a set rule for how often and long we pray to God. We must "pray without ceasing" (1 Thess. 5:17), "at all times in the Spirit" (Eph. 6:18), and sometimes suddenly because of need (Num. 12:13; Neh. 2:4–5). Daniel apparently had specific times to pray (Dan. 6:10). Our Lord "would withdraw to desolate places and pray" (Luke 5:16). We may not have an explicit command to pray a certain amount each day or at a certain time, but we must pray. William Bates makes the following analogy: "If the bird leaves her nest for a long space, the eggs chill and are not fit for production; but where there is a constant incubation, then they bring forth: so when we leave religious duties for a long space, our affections chill, and grow cold; and are not fit to produce holiness, and comfort to our souls."[11] This is eminently true of prayer.

10. Winslow refers to a converted heathen's saying something to this effect. See *Personal Declension*, 113.

11. William Bates, *The Whole Works of the Rev. William Bates*, 4 vols. (London: For James Black, 1815), 3:125.

The Lord knows that prayer is a challenge, which is a reason why we have so many different motivations to pray (e.g., personal need, aid to assurance, salvation of souls, Christ's glory). So why do backsliders neglect prayer? Often it is because they feel that they are getting along just fine without God in their lives. One of the ways in which God motivates us to pray is by promising to bless us as a result, even reward us—though not meritoriously but graciously. God who grants the grace to pray graciously crowns his own with gifts.

Our Father in heaven knows how to give good gifts to his children (Matt. 7:11; Luke 11:1–13), for "every good gift and every perfect gift is from above, coming down from the Father of lights, with whom there is no variation or shadow due to change" (James 1:17). We have access, through Christ, by the Spirit, to a generous Father. But we sometimes get into a rut and find it difficult to pray. At first, we don't give up prayer altogether, yet get more and more comfortable neglecting it before ignoring God almost completely while uttering a word here and there (e.g., at the dinner table with the family) to appease our conscience. We can often give up frequent prayer because we see no change in our outward circumstances. Thus, there is no burden to seek God, because all appears to still be well with material needs, despite the command to offer daily petitions: "Give us this day our daily bread" (Matt. 6:11).

God promises rewards to his children. In what is commonly called the "Lord's Prayer," Jesus says that "your Father who sees in secret will reward you" (Matt. 6:6). Unbelief keeps us from prayer, but tied to that, we fail to believe the promise that he rewards us with that which is so good that we cannot afford not to ask him. We would rather seek what we can see from the world than the promises from God. We do not have because we do not ask, and we do not ask because we lack faith in God and his promises (21:22).

By faith, believing that God exists, we know that he rewards those who seek him (Heb. 11:6). But lack of faith leads to lack of prayer, which leads to a lack of good things from God. All because we fail to ask with the frequency and fervency that such gracious promises demand. Jesus was not ignorant of his rewards and the promises that were the basis for such rewards. In one place he explicitly asks for what is promised: "And now, Father, glorify me in your own presence with the glory that I had with you before the world existed" (John 17:5).

We do not always know precisely how the Lord will reward us for what we do in secret, but God no doubt answers our prayers in ways that are sometimes indescribable. We receive wondrous answers and often ask ourselves why we don't ask more often. There is no lack in God, but (sadly) we lack desire to receive from him. Sometimes God rewards us by not giving us what we ask, because we ask with wrong motives (James 4:3). There are also prayers that God answers, but not in our own lifetime. Think of Stephen's prayer in Acts 7:59–60, which likely resulted in the conversion of Saul of Tarsus. Incredibly, Moses' desire to see God's glory (Ex. 33:18) was gloriously answered on the Mount of Transfiguration (Matt. 17:1–3). God "is able to do far more abundantly than all that we ask or think" (Eph. 3:20).

Backsliders, however, are often people who do not experience much outward loss. They have jobs that pay, families that love, and friends that care. They have stable lives with enjoyable hobbies, yet are ignorant of the fact that their spiritual stability is crumbling or that they are in for a "rude awakening" from God. A positive cure for prayerlessness can be the desire to receive rewards from God. But when this fails, sometimes a "negative" cure is required.

As sons of God, we are treated accordingly. God always blesses his children, but sometimes that blessing comes in the form of discipline. And we should not "regard lightly the discipline of the Lord" because he disciplines out of love (Heb. 12:5–6). When we drift, and stop "familiar conversation" with God, sometimes he brings various trials or sufferings into our lives because he is treating us as his children (v. 7). If God did not discipline us, he would not be a loving Father and we would be "illegitimate children" (v. 8). Thankfully, God's discipline works and "yields the peaceful fruit of righteousness to those who have been trained by it" (v. 11). Brooks points out that God can "look sourly, chide bitterly, and strike heavily, even where, and when he loves dearly."[12]

What is the point of God's discipline? It may have several uses, such as stopping us from willfully committing certain sins. But ultimately, discipline leads us back into close communion with our loving Father. Prayerless backsliders fail to seek the good that comes from the hand of God and must sometimes experience the "bad" from that same hand. In this way, they are meant to see that living apart from God is emptiness. Anyone with even a cursory knowledge of the Psalms knows how often David was driven to the Lord during trials and even chastisements (see, e.g., Ps. 38).

Henry Scougal, author of the well-known work *The Life of God in the Soul of Man*, wrote a sermon called "The Necessity and Advantage of Early Afflictions." It is a pastoral masterpiece, in part because he personally knew well the value of suffering in the Christian life. Scougal notes that God orders things for our happiness and uses the best means to accomplish this end. When we wander or begin a path of backsliding, God aims to restore us by "milder and more gentle methods: he tries our gratitude . . . by all the endearments of mercy and goodness; he draws us with cords of love."[13] But if we persist in our backsliding and abuse his goodness toward us, turning his grace into an excuse for licentiousness, "then not only his justice, but his love to us, not only his hatred to sin, but his affection to us, will oblige him to alter his method, and

12. Brooks, *Precious Remedies against Satan's Devices*, 193.
13. Henry Scougal, *Works of the Rev. Henry Scougal* (Glasgow: William Collins, 1830), 170.

take the rod in his hand, and try what severity can do."[14] When the rod strikes us, we very often fall down before God in prayer and return to him. Does not our personal experience sadly testify to these realities? We should be constrained by love, but sometimes he must constrain us with pain, yet never apart from love.

Corporate Prayer

Prayer is difficult, so we need each other to encourage it. Since we can enter the holy places through Christ's blood, we can draw near with full assurance because we have been cleansed (Heb. 10:19–22). After affirming these truths, the author exhorts his hearers to "stir up one another to love and good works" (v. 24). This cannot happen if we neglect meeting together (v. 25). Backsliders drift from God, as evidenced by pulling away from his people.

As a pastor, I am amazed at the drive that many Christians have —including myself!—for doing things that are not particularly of much eternal significance. Those pursuits may not be wrong in and of themselves, but our zeal for and prioritizing them is often misplaced, especially if they keep us from corporate prayer and seeking first the kingdom of God (Matt. 6:33). Why is it that meeting together with fellow Christians once a week (or even once a month) is so difficult?

There has been a proliferation of books on the gospel and "grace-centered" this or that in recent years. If indeed there has been a recapturing of the beauties of the gospel of God, then should we not expect a recapturing of the beauties of corporate prayer? At such times, we cry out for such gospel grace in our lives and the lives of others, which includes those without Christ. So why does corporate prayer suffer in the Western church today?

14. Scougal, 170.

It may be partly the pastor's fault. He does not see the importance of prayer, and it comes through in his ministry. Or the prayer
meetings are a little trite and there's a fear of opening one's heart
to others (see 2 Cor. 6:11). We freely bring up the health needs
of others, from the common cold to cancer, but fail to ask for
encouragement in dealing with wayward children or a particular
besetting sin. It is not that the first is wrongly included, but that the
second is wrongly omitted. Naturally, we ought to show wisdom
in our requests, but we are far too safe with each other, and so
we end up (perhaps unconsciously) seeing little point in praying
together. Sometimes we can slip into a form of hyper-Calvinism
or, worse, fatalism: God will accomplish his purposes, and he will
do so whether I ask or not.

But while these reasons may all be true to some extent, the
real reason why we do not pray together is that we have not experienced in power the holiness, wisdom, and goodness of God in
personal prayer. Perhaps many have not had any real experience
of his goodness in their personal communion, which means that
they are unmotivated to pray with others. The public problem
typically begins in private. Yet sometimes the way to "excite" our
private prayer life is through the encouragement of public prayer.
The two feed off each other.

Those enjoying communion with the triune God should want
it for others, and so meet with their brothers and sisters to pray.
As a body, we thrive in unity and in numbers (Matt. 18:20; Acts
1:14). We can encourage others not only by praying with them and
for them, but also by speaking of the goodness of God in our lives.

Those of us who go for runs often do not feel like doing so.
Usually, after a while, the run gets easier, and we experience satisfaction when we finish. Prayer is very much like that. Winslow
says that prayer is not just a "solemn duty to be observed, but also
a precious privilege to be enjoyed. Happy is that believer, when

duties come to be viewed as privileges."[15] What a blessing it is to rise from one's knees after meeting with the Lord; the assurance we receive is more precious than gold.

To keep us from backsliding, God in his Word has encouraged praying together. Hearing a child call upon God as his or her Father soothes our own souls as adults. Hearing a father plead for greater faithfulness in his own household reinforces the struggle that many experience as leaders of families. As we pray, God's kingdom is advanced. Little wonder that corporate prayer was a hallmark of early Christian piety (Acts 2:42).

Satan hates private prayer, but it may be that he hates corporate prayer even more. One soldier fighting can do some damage to the enemy, but there is strength in numbers. The devil cannot stand to see Christians praying together because he knows that it will not only advance God's kingdom (and destroy his own) but likely also keep them from turning from God. Sadly, Satan seems to win some of the battles when churches are busy about many things (e.g., programs for kids) but lack a robust corporate prayer life.

Application

In his sermon "Hypocrites Deficient in the Duty of Prayer," Jonathan Edwards highlights how hypocrites may for a season call upon God in prayer, but eventually fail to continue. Secret prayer can be omitted by them while they slide into apostasy, without the notice of others and while apparently in good standing in the church. By way of application, Edwards argues that professing Christians who fail to pray at all can throw away their hope.[16] Giving up prayer altogether is a sign not just of backsliding, but perhaps of apostasy.

15. Winslow, *Personal Declension*, 116.
16. Jonathan Edwards, *The Works of President Edwards*, 4 vols. (New York: Leavitt & Allen, 1856), 4:479.

Edwards notes that backsliders have one rule for themselves and another for others: "They can make larger allowances for themselves," says Edwards, "than they can for others" in terms of the various ways we disobey.[17] But if they do not love God and Christ above all, including their earthly friends, with whom they frequently speak, then they are testing the Lord. Edwards adds that it is the "nature of love to be averse to absence," and so to neglect prayer and communion with God "seems to be inconsistent with supreme love to God."[18] Paul clearly declares to us: "If anyone has no love for the Lord, let him be accursed. Our Lord, come!" (1 Cor. 16:22).

To ignore someone and claim to love that person is inconsistent with the nature of love. Love binds together; hatred separates. True love leads to union, satisfaction, and goodwill between the parties involved. If you claim to love God but hate to speak to him as he desires and enables you to speak with him, you are either a backslider or a hypocrite. These are strong words, but the Scriptures do not allow, among the truly converted, indifference toward communion with the triune God. The love of the Father, the grace of the Lord Jesus Christ, and the fellowship of the Spirit are not mere options for the Christian, but rather our very lifeblood. We are united to the triune God, which cannot but mean sweet communion. As the hymn goes:

> Yet she on earth hath union
> with God the Three in One,
> and mystic sweet communion
> with those whose rest is won:
> O happy ones and holy!

17. Edwards, 4:480.
18. Edwards, 4:481.

Lord, give us grace that we,
like them, the meek and lowly,
on high may dwell with thee.[19]

Our solution to our lack of prayer is to pray, not only privately but corporately. It may be that your renewal of the latter will stir up the former. In addition, make use of the typical opportunities to pray: before a meal, upon going to sleep, when waking up, and so on, in order to keep communion with God as frequent as possible, even if your prayers are shorter and more spontaneous. By God's grace, for the backslider, perhaps such prayers will lead to more vigorous, sustained, lively private prayer. And as God answers our prayers—as he has promised to do!—we will, by his grace, see that we cannot afford to ignore him.

For Further Reflection

1. Which is most neglected in the church and in your own personal life: private or corporate prayer? Why do you think that is?
2. What have been some of the best encouragements for you to continue in prayer, whether private or corporate?
3. What should one do if he or she feels prayerless?
4. Read and meditate on Daniel 9:1–19; Matthew 6:1–15.

19. Samuel J. Stone, "The Church's One Foundation" (1866).

10

The Disregard for Scripture

*How often in the reading of [the Bible] do we meet with, and are
as it were surprised with, gracious words, that enlighten, quicken,
comfort, endear, and engage our souls! How often do we find sin
wounded, grace encouraged, faith excited, love inflamed, and this in
that endless variety of inward frames and outward occasions which
we are liable unto!* (John Owen)[1]

The Happy Man

Think about how much information we take in daily in all
areas of life. Most of us are probably users of social media, perhaps even addicts wanting relief from the oppressive and endless
scrolling. Besides that, we are often speaking with others, reading,
watching television, or listening to music. Even as we drive, we
are taking information in. The list goes on and on. We are also
inundated with lies from the world, whether in the news or false
advertising. Additionally, sometimes we are told things that are

---

1. John Owen, *The Works of John Owen*, ed. W. H. Goold, 24 vols. (Edinburgh:
T&T Clark, 1850–53), 4:192.

unkind or harsh. What hope is there to navigate a world where our best interests are often not considered by others or where so much falsehood abounds?

Reading God's Word in freedom and privacy at home is a privilege that many Christians do not have, and many who have such a privilege take it for granted. Some in areas of persecution and restriction must be exceedingly careful not to be caught with Bibles or even portions of God's Word. If you are reading this book, you almost certainly have many Christian books and several Bibles in your homes. Not all Christians are blessed with such privileges. And with such privileges come responsibilities. There is a woeful lack of Bible knowledge in the church today. This refers not to new Christians who are just learning, but to "seasoned" Christians, pastors, and professors of theology who know so little of God's Word, and have a scarcity of wisdom to go along with it, that the truth they do know changes their lives very little.

In terms of personal, practical religion, reading God's Word and prayer stand out as two of the most important things one can do to maintain a consistent walk with the Lord. As J. C. Ryle said with regard to the value of the Bible: "Happy is that man who possesses a Bible! Happier still is he who reads it! Happiest of all is he who not only reads it, but obeys it, and makes it the rule of his faith and practice!"[2]

Backsliders usually give up personal Bible reading. They may go through the motions occasionally and do a bit of reading here and there to appease their consciences, but they lack any real hunger for the Bible or joy in communing with God through his Word. They lack desire to know God, and instead of addressing the issue, they give up.

---

2. J. C. Ryle, *Practical Religion: Being Plain Papers on the Daily Duties, Experience, Dangers, and Privileges of Professing Christians* (London: Charles Murray, 1900), 97.

We need not know J. R. R. Tolkien or William Shakespeare to be very fine Christians. But we cannot be ignorant of God's Word and expect to live a healthy Christian life. In restricted countries, persecution keeps believers close to God with whatever portion of the Bible (sometimes very little) they have. The Bible should be our number-one priority in terms of reading. We should aim to master its contents, not just a few "life verses" here and there. I have examined candidates for the ministry for fifteen years now in the Presbyterian Church in America, and Bible knowledge is often the weakest area among candidates who wish to be teachers of the Word.

Thomas Goodwin, a first-class theologian in his era, read widely. Yet his own son said of his father: "But the Scriptures were what he most studied."[3] Would our children say the same? What do we most study? That is a question that all Christians must ask of themselves. Backsliders, for whom the answer to that question is almost certainly "Not the Bible," may not even have time to consider the question. Their neglect of God's Word, however, goes a long way in explaining their spiritual state.

Don't Be Ignorant

The evidence from God's Word on the importance and value of the Scriptures is overwhelming. For example, when the Sadducees

---

3. Thomas Goodwin, *The Works of Thomas Goodwin*, 12 vols. (Edinburgh: James Nichol, 1861–66; repr., Grand Rapids: Reformation Heritage Books, 2006), 2:lxxiv. John Owen says that the most "deplorable mistake" made by theologians, including preachers, is their "diversion from an immediate, direct study of the Scriptures themselves unto the studying of commentators, critics, scholiasts, annotators, and the like helps.... Not that I condemn the use and study of them, which I wish men were more diligent in, but desire pardon if I mistake, ... by the experience of my own folly for many years, that many which seriously study the things of God do yet rather make it their business to inquire after the sense of other men on the Scriptures than to search studiously into them themselves." Owen, *Works*, 4:213.

asked him about the resurrection, our Lord responded, "You are wrong, because you know neither the Scriptures nor the power of God" (Matt. 22:29). He expected them to know the Bible. Certainly, mere Bible reading can be dangerous if it is misunderstood or distorted. God's people must be concerned not only with what he says, but also with what he means. Growing in the grace and knowledge of Christ does not occur merely by reading the Bible individually, but involves the broader context of other believers in the church especially, where ordained pastors are gifts given from the hand of Christ to feed the sheep. But other tools can be helpful, such as study Bibles, commentaries, books, confessions, and catechisms. These help Christians grow in their understanding of God's Word.

Make no mistake, the reading of God's Word must have a priority in our lives individually and corporately. If the Word is not prioritized in corporate worship, its leaders should expect members to pay little regard to it individually or in families. To live faithfully in this world, with courage, we need God's Word. The Lord told Joshua three times to be strong and courageous (Josh. 1:5–9) while reminding him: "This Book of the Law shall not depart from your mouth, but you shall meditate on it day and night, so that you may be careful to do according to all that is written in it. For then you will make your way prosperous, and then you will have good success" (v. 8). There is a command and a promise: if Joshua meditates on God's Word and obeys it, he will be successful. That promise, in a sense, rings true for all of us as Christians, not just Joshua.

Israel's kings, when they were enthroned, were commanded to write in a book a copy of God's law (likely Deut. 1–30; see 31:9). This law was to be approved by the Levitical priests. Then the law would be with the king, and he was to read it "all the days of his life, that he may learn to fear the Lord his God by keeping all the words of this law and these statutes, and doing them, that his heart may not be lifted up above his brothers, and that he may not turn aside from the commandment, either to the right hand or to the left, so that he may continue long in his kingdom, he and his children, in Israel" (17:19–20). Reading God's Word should lead to keeping it, and then receiving blessings from above. Already in Deuteronomy 6, we note how the importance of God's Word has relevance for families, not just individuals such as kings (6:7–9).

Priests were to be men of the Word of God. Ezra is perhaps the finest example: "For Ezra had set his heart to study the Law of the LORD, and to do it and to teach his statutes and rules in Israel" (Ezra 7:10). Ezra was a faithful priest, in no small part because he internalized what he read. And prophets were obviously to be men who knew God's Word, for they were his mouthpieces, forthtelling to God's people his commandments, promises, and warnings. As Jeremiah declares:

> Your words were found, and I ate them,
>   and your words became to me a joy
>   and the delight of my heart,
> for I am called by your name,
>   O LORD, God of hosts. (Jer. 15:16)

The Old Testament prophets searched God's Word intently, with the Spirit of Christ in them, in order to see Christ's sufferings and glories (1 Peter 1:10–12).

As a Prophet, Priest, and King, our Lord was the Man of God's Word *par excellence*. The Old Testament Scriptures dripped from his mouth. In his wilderness temptation, Satan appealed to him, "If you are the Son of God, command this stone to become bread" (Luke 4:3). Likely starving after forty days without food, emaciated, and his body crying out for nourishment, Jesus answered the devil's temptation with words from Deuteronomy 8:3: "It is written, 'Man shall not live by bread alone'" (Luke 4:4). People often think that Jesus chose spiritual food instead of natural food. But his response gets to a more fundamental issue. In Deuteronomy, the Israelites were taught that God takes care of them, apart from purely natural means. Jesus appealed to God's Word to prove that he would live by faith, depending not on his own resources but on his Father's powerful hand. God's Word proves repeatedly that we can depend on him to live the life of faith when the life of sight may be more appealing. Will we trust him or lean on our own resources and understanding? Ignorance of God's Word fuels unbelief, whereas knowledge of the Scriptures gives strength to faith.

In the Gospel accounts, Jesus regularly asks the question, "Have you not read . . . ?" In Matthew's Gospel, for example, he asks the question several times (12:3, 5; 19:4; 21:16, 42; 22:31). This question appears to come from the lips of Christ more than any other question he asks. Not reading and understanding was a problem among religious people back in Christ's day, and it is still a problem today in our churches.

We need to be like Job and say, "I have not departed from the commandment of his lips; I have treasured the words of his mouth more than my portion of food" (Job 23:12). Or consider the Jews in Berea, who were "more noble than those in Thessalonica; they received the word with all eagerness, examining the Scriptures daily to see if these things were so" (Acts 17:11). As newborn infants crave milk, so Christians must crave "the pure spiritual milk" of God's Word so that we can "grow up into salvation" (1 Peter 2:2). The word used by Peter for "grow up" is in the passive. The idea is that the milk of God's Word (see 1:23–25) will give growth to the believer who drinks in the nourishment that God's truth offers. As John Bunyan aptly observed in applying this text, "All God's children are criers"; they cannot be quiet unless they "have a bellyful of the milk of God's Word."[4]

---

4. John Bunyan, "Mr. Bunyan's Last Sermon," in *The Select Works of John Bunyan* [. . .] (Glasgow, Edinburgh, and London: William Collins, Sons, and Company, 1866), 775.

Application

John Angell James, a pastor-theologian whose words I wish we read more of today, wrote an essay, "On Books," which is a delightful survey of book suggestions to his readers in practically every field of study. But before he begins his suggestions, he remarks: "Whatever books you neglect, then, my children, neglect not the Bible. Whatever books you read, read this. Let not a day pass without perusing some portion of holy writ."[5] I am not convinced that a Christian has sinned if he or she does not read God's Word each day. Life is complex, and there are times when we may fail to read God's Word on any given day. Moreover, some can read the Bible each day but with little profit to their souls, simply because they have gone through the motions of reading God's Word without seeking him in the process. Notwithstanding these points, we should make it our aim to be in God's Word daily and stop making excuses for not doing so. Most of us imbibe so much from the world and social media that we are severely tempting ourselves to sin if we are not buttressing our souls daily with God's Word. Whether in the morning or in the evening, whether many chapters or a few verses, the Christian needs daily careful and prayerful consideration of God's truth. One can indeed get more out of a single verse than many chapters, but that in no way means to read less instead of more.

Backsliding Christians are not those who lack a Bible. They are those who lack a love for the Bible. And sadly, lacking a love for the Bible is to lack love for God. We commune with God in various ways. We can pray, meditate, sing, and so on. But reading God's Word allows God to objectively speak to us. We can respond not only with prayer and thanksgiving, but also with a life well lived for his glory. When this happens, we know that our living well for

5. John Angell James, *The Christian Father's Present to His Children* (New York: R. Carter, 1853), 219.

God results from the power of his Word in our lives. Jesus prayed, "Sanctify them in the truth; your word is truth" (John 17:17). Our sanctification cannot happen apart from the Word doing its work. To the degree that we rob ourselves of the truth, we will be robbing ourselves of the sanctifying power of God's truth.

Backsliders stop reading God's Word because they really don't see the value in it. They know it well enough, as far as they are concerned, and have no desire to go beyond that. In sinful unbelief, they do not seek God in his Word and have no desire to be in God's presence or experience his power. Some simply fear the presence of God, even as the Danish philosopher Søren Kierkegaard admitted: "To be alone with Holy Scripture! I dare not!"[6] Why would that be? Because once we read God's Word, we may just have to question the patterns of our life. Kierkegaard speaks of how God encounters and confronts a person in the words of the Bible: "Have you done what you read there? And then, then—yes, then I am trapped. Then either straightaway into actions—or immediately a humbling admission."[7]

The backslider thinks it's safer to stay away from God's Word because it avoids discomfort. If you are a true believer, you understand this temptation, but also realize how horribly perilous such a mentality is to the Christian life and so avoid such neglect.

One way to preserve a love for the Bible is to read with others —for example, in family worship. Regardless, such times should seek to stir up the desire for truth and not be dull and tiresome. I have witnessed the drudgery of a father's reading monotonously in front of an uninterested audience and felt that the audience was somewhat justified because of the rather boring way in which family worship was being led.

---

6. Søren Kierkegaard, *For Self-Examination / Judge for Yourself!*, ed. and trans. Howard V. Hong and Edna H. Hong (Princeton, NJ: Princeton University Press, 2015), 31.

7. Kierkegaard, 31.

The Bible should be explained and taught in a way that would cause someone to want to read more of it. Younger children cannot be expected to merely go and read their Bibles alone. As they get older, they can do so, but in connection with the instruction they have received at home and at church. Likewise, their delight in reading the Word will be impacted by parents whose own excitement over God's Word is palpable.

John Newton speaks well concerning Bible reading:

> I know not a better rule of reading the Scripture, than to read it through from beginning to end; and, when we have finished it once, to begin it again . . . : provided we pray to him who has the keys to open our understandings, and to anoint our eyes with his spiritual eye-salve! . . . Experience alone, can prove the advantage of this method, if steadily persevered in. To make a few efforts, and then give over, is like taking a few steps and then standing still, which would do little toward completing a long journey. But though a person walked slowly, and but a little way in a day, if he walked every day, and with his face always in the same direction, year after year, he would in time travel over the globe! By thus traveling patiently and steadily through the Scripture, and repeating our progress, we would increase in Scriptural knowledge to the end of life.[8]

This is the essence of faithful Christian living, namely, a tough, patient, long walk to life eternal, but one filled with faith, hope, and love toward our faithful God and Savior.

Finally, the devil hates God's Word because it was implanted in Christ's heart and assured him that he must die for our sins. Our Lord said to his disciples: "For I tell you that this Scripture must

---

8. John Newton, *The Works of John Newton*, 4 vols. (New Haven, CT: Nathan Whiting, 1824), 4:466.

be fulfilled in me: 'And he was numbered with the transgressors.' For what is written about me has its fulfillment" (Luke 22:37, quoting Isa. 53:12). What else did God's Word teach Christ? That after suffering would come glory: "Was it not necessary that the Christ should suffer these things and enter into his glory?" (Luke 24:26). Just as our Lord needed the promises of God's Word to help him walk in obedience to his Father, so we also must be filled with God's promises found in the Scriptures that will carry us to glory. To quote John Angell James again, "Whatever books you neglect, then, my children, neglect not the Bible."

For Further Reflection

1. What keeps you from reading your Bible?
2. What keeps you from reading your Bible well?
3. How can we cultivate better Bible reading habits?
4. Do you ever spend time meditating on just a verse or two? If not, why not?
5. Read and meditate on Psalm 119; Luke 24:13–27.

11

The Abandonment of Church

Set your heart on the communion of saints. Men hardly forsake
what they love. (William Gouge)[1]

Public before Private

Corporate worship should be prioritized more than any other
Christian duty. The gathering at church of the redeemed on the
Lord's Day is where the best blessings are received and where we
dialogue with the triune God in ways that private communion
cannot offer. Shepherds, gifted by Christ (Eph. 4:11), take care
of the sheep by speaking to them the voice of God (Acts 20:28;
1 Thess. 2:13), knowing that they together hear his voice and
follow the Chief Shepherd (John 10:27).

All true corporate worship is heavenly worship, and such is
the acknowledgment of Christ as Lord of all (Rev. 5). In corporate
worship we ascend to heaven (Heb. 12:22–24), surrounded by
angels and saints in glory; and we fall before the throne of Christ,

1. William Gouge, *A Commentary on the Whole Epistle to the Hebrews* [. . .], vol. 2
(Edinburgh: James Nichol, 1866), 336.

who is seated in glory at the right hand of the Father (Rev. 4:2; 5:1, 8–14). Much worship today intoxicates people with the "drug" of entertainment, emotionalism, or self-gratification, which loses its potency for many people, whose "fix" no longer works the way it once did and who eventually pull away. Worship must be first and foremost a meeting with the risen Christ on his terms. If church is a meeting to hear one's favorite preacher, what happens if God removes him or he moves to a "bigger, better church"?

All over the world, and since the beginning of time, God has gathered his people to worship him publicly and thereby glorify his name. We are called into the presence of the triune God, coming to the Father in the name of Christ by the power of the Spirit so that we can worship acceptably in reverence and awe (Heb. 12:28). As we truly commune with him, along with our brothers and sisters in the Lord, we will be blessed, not only by God but also by the saints. If we come seeking something other than the Lord, we worship with our mouths only and not our hearts, which are distant from God (Isa. 29:13). Yet we have every reason to come to him ultimately for him, for that is why Christ died (1 Peter 3:18).

Calls to worship together abound in God's Word (see Ps. 100). For example, in Psalm 95:6–7, we read:

> Oh come, let us worship and bow down;
>> let us kneel before the LORD, our Maker!
> For he is our God,
>> and we are the people of his pasture,
>> and the sheep of his hand.

The New Testament reinforces this emphasis: "They devoted themselves to the apostles' teaching and the fellowship, to the breaking of bread and the prayers.... And day by day, attending the temple together and breaking bread in their homes, they received their food with glad and generous hearts, praising God and having favor with all the people. And the Lord added to their number day by day those who were being saved" (Acts 2:42, 46–47). Devotion to the Lord was never meant to be a solitary pursuit.

Christian persecution most often arises in the context of the church, where faithful corporate worship is both public and audible. This is true whether in New Testament times or today in parts of such countries as Nigeria and China. Typically, Christians are persecuted not because they avoid public worship by secretly meeting alone with the Lord behind closed doors but when their worship is seen and heard by a hostile world. Even in restricted or hostile nations where Christians gather secretly, they are still seeking to do so corporately.

David Clarkson, a Puritan copastor with John Owen in the seventeenth century, argued in a sermon that public worship takes precedence over that which is private, based on Psalm 87:2: "the LORD loves the gates of Zion more than all the dwelling places of Jacob."[2] In this "backsliding age," many professing Christians cheapen the importance and value of the local church, thinking that the church is a negotiable when it comes to faithful Christianity. Many who abandon corporate worship, attend even somewhat regularly without joining, or join without taking public vows of membership seriously want to imagine that private Christianity is what matters and that the public aspect is not necessary even if it is a nice option at times. This not only is a sign of gross ignorance concerning what the Scriptures teach but reveals a backsliding heart. Such a person wants religion on his or her own terms, not God's.

Christians making corporate worship a priority seek God's blessing and with his armor protect themselves from backsliding. But those who disregard the public gathering of the saints run into

---

2. David Clarkson, *The Practical Works of David Clarkson*, 3 vols. (Edinburgh: James Nichol, 1865), 3:187.

the world without the armor of God in their fight (or lack thereof) against their sin, the devil, and the world.

Public worship is to be preferred over private for many good reasons. For example, God is more glorified in public worship because public glory is better than private glory (Ps. 96:1–3).[3] Promises of God's special presence are made to two or three gathered together (Matt. 18:20). Christ's gifts to the church are many and include public ordinances and officers. The Lord's Supper is a corporate fellowship meal, necessarily involving the body of Christ, not just an individual in it (1 Cor. 11:29). God has appointed preachers to publicly encourage, exhort, explain, and apply the Word of God and, in so doing, enrich the people of God. Private worshipers miss out on this, even in some sense when watching a streamed or recorded sermon. They become their own instructors, not needing the teachers that Christ gave the church (Eph. 4:8–13). They resist oversight from undershepherds (Heb. 13:17) and, in the process (however ignorantly they do it), the Chief Shepherd himself (1 Peter 2:25; 5:4). Moreover, at public worship, we can and must do others good, as we "stir up one another to love and good works, [by] not neglecting to meet together, as is the habit of some" (Heb. 10:24–25). Public worship allows us to encourage our brethren, and receive encouragement in return (v. 25).

Backsliders might not stop going to church totally, but very often they do not make the Lord's Day or worship on it a priority. The zeal they lack for the Lord they possess in abundance in their excuses for missing church. They love corporate worship far less than sports fans (which may include them) idolize their favorite team. The zeal of sports fans at stadiums is a sight to behold. Neither cold weather nor sickness keeps them from being present to cheer on their team, whereas backsliders quickly give in to excuses (sometimes pitiful) to miss worship.

3. Clarkson, 3:189.

Often their excuses concern the failure of fellow Christians and officers of the church to live up to their calling. Indeed, the Lord's people have not always acted blamelessly, and many pastors have been unfaithful in their teaching or conduct. But let us not forget that the Lord, infinitely more than anyone else, received unloving and unfair treatment from and endured unfaithfulness in the people of God. Yet that did not keep him from loving the church. He alone had reasons to abandon us all, but he won the ungodly by his love, patience, and faithfulness.

Backsliders who make such allegations do so hypocritically in refusing to admit their own failures while they point out the hypocrisy of others. Hypocrisy in the church should not be a reason to stop attending, for the following reasons: First, only God, not any of us (thankfully!), knows who the real hypocrites are. Second, our presence in the body allows us to live, act, and worship in such a way that we can help (and possibly win over) these alleged hypocrites. Third, we can always make good use of all people in our conformity to Christ, even our enemies, whom we are called to bear with in love (Luke 6:35).

Areas of Danger

Some obvious areas of danger typically lead to backsliding in corporate worship on the Lord's Day. Many students go off to college without giving sufficient attention to their spiritual care (this may include their parents), especially in an academic setting hostile to the Christian faith. When many students go to college, they do not simply leave home but leave the church as well. Many young Christians have gone off to the "far country" (college) and have been left to themselves to fight the good fight, only to find out that their strength diminishes rather quickly. Parents can even send their child to an ostensibly Christian college without a good church nearby, which mitigates the value of the school.

A further area of backsliding can occur among younger Christians whose parents allow them to miss corporate worship because of activities such as sports. As a pastor significantly involved at a Christian school where I also coach high school soccer, I am amazed at how many students regularly miss church and are meagerly involved in the life of the congregation. Why? Many parents and students openly admit, without any apparent shame or embarrassment, that Sunday soccer matches make it "impossible" to attend. Instead of singing, "Praise God from whom all blessings flow," they are cheering their team or yelling at a referee or an opposing player.

The next generation of Christians are being told, either implicitly or explicitly, by the actions of their parents, that corporate worship is not very important. So the downgrade begins, and little wonder that so many grandparents wake up to the shocking reality that if their grandchildren are going to get any Christian religious instruction, it will have to come from them because their own children seem uninterested in making church attendance a priority. Many grandparents live with some regret that they themselves did not make worship a priority, and now they are seeing the effects of such spiritual slovenliness over the course of generations.

Few backsliding Christians who stop devoting themselves to various public means of grace admit that they are sinning. They have a litany of excuses lined up when pressed by a faithful brother or sister. Many times, instead of admitting a moral failure in their life, they will have so-called intellectual reasons for their abandonment of the church.

Archibald Alexander refers to various types of formerly professing Christians who abandon the faith and commit apostasy. He identifies various reasons for why people apostatize from the faith, including those who, because of pride, "forsake the true doctrines of the gospel, and fall in love with some flattering, flesh-pleasing form of heresy; and spend their time in zealous efforts to over-throw that very truth, which they once professed to prize."[4] Today, we might see this in what has been popularly called *evangelical deconstructionism*. This slippery term can mean different things in different contexts (e.g., academic or popular).

This philosophical label is sometimes used by evangelicals who have a crisis of faith because their experience of truth does not seem to hold up to established orthodoxy. For example, a young evangelical may go off to college and meet people who are homosexual, and then start to wonder whether these people are really sinning against the Lord, since they appear to be kind, gen-erous, and hospitable. Over time, the young man or woman will often deconstruct the faith that he or she was taught and grew up with, and perhaps even abandon Christian orthodoxy altogether. Often there is a shallow basis for such people's beliefs, an anemic gospel, and a faulty understanding of God's Word. Thus, when these young people's faith is attacked, they are able to respond with only the measly amount of truth that was taught to them.

At first, they claim to merely be "cleaning up a few things," and even strenuously affirm their continued allegiance to the person of Christ. Soon enough, however, an unraveling of their new belief system leaves very little room for their former orthodox Chris-tianity, which makes little sense to them anymore. Experience, not Christ, becomes their lord.

This new movement in evangelicalism is hardly new, in a certain sense. The abandonment of the truth has a sad history, beginning with the devil and Adam, and continuing among the people of God ever since. But today many who reject the church and renege on the vows they made will offer "theological" reasons for their practice.

---

4. Archibald Alexander, *Thoughts on Religious Experience* (Philadelphia: Presbyterian Board of Publication, 1841), 205.

The person who feels that he or she is not hearing the gospel preached and the Word delivered faithfully in all the elements of worship may have legitimate reasons to find a place where the Scriptures truly shape the life of the church. But such a person doesn't abandon the church altogether. Rather, he or she seeks a place where faithfulness—not sinlessness—abounds. One may have a legitimate concern about a local body, but after persistent efforts to seek Christ's honor are rejected by the leadership, the truly faithful person will find a place where he or she can honor the Lord. Yet censorious people who make a big deal of problems in the church to justify their absence and so abandon the church have serious heart problems above and beyond any supposed convictions to defend or godly honor to uphold.

If anyone had reasons to abandon the church, it was our Lord. Unlike us, he truly was sinless and so could point the finger at everyone else except himself. Instead, he laid down his life for his bride and won her by his love, faithfulness, and truth. Jesus loved the church, "warts and all," so that we might have the same attitude as that of our Savior. Paul's mindset toward the Corinthians is instructive on this point. We might read 1 Corinthians with some bewilderment, but in 2 Corinthians we see the heart of the apostle wide open toward those whom he counts as Christ's sheep and thus worth the pain and effort (2 Cor. 6:11–13).

Application

There are few more worrying questions that children can ask their parents than "Do we have to go to church?" or "Are we going to church this week?" These are the questions that emerge from doubt over a practice that should be beyond doubt. Two indisputable truths should characterize every Christian parent-child relationship: children should know that their parents love them, and their parents love Christ more. This will mean that corporate worship on the Lord's Day comes first, not Johnny's baseball game or Lydia's soccer travel team, if there is a conflict. True love to them cannot compete with true love for God. A parent who chooses God first shows his or her child true love, since the best love that we can show our children is the love whereby God has no competitor.

When we think of church on the Lord's Day, we should not think so much about going to church—though we do in fact do that—but rather that we are going to worship God with our brothers and sisters in Christ in the power of the Spirit and on a day that the Lord has given for our good. The Lord's Day is a foretaste of the everlasting Sabbath rest awaiting the people of God (Heb. 4:9), a day of worship and rest in the glorious freedom we have in Christ from the cares of this life. We are going to the place where we are blessed by God, are fed by him in Word and sacrament, and are able to bless others. It is possible to backslide despite faithful church attendance. But those who do not make worship a consistent priority will backslide. When a person refuses good food, the effects over time are obvious. This is eminently true when it comes to refusing the nourishment of the church.

Protestants have historically spoken of the absolute necessity of serving in the local, visible church. We join with Cyprian in saying that the church "keeps us for God."[5] He adds: "She appoints the sons whom she has born for the kingdom. Whoever is separated from the Church and is joined to an adulteress, is separated from the promises of the Church; nor can he who forsakes the Church of Christ attain to the rewards of Christ. He is a stranger; he is profane; he is an enemy. He can no longer have God for his Father, who has not the Church for his mother."[6] This is what we

5. Cyprian, *Treatise on the Unity of the Church*, in *The Ante-Nicene Fathers*, ed. Alexander Roberts and James Donaldson (New York: Charles Scribner's Sons, 1908), 5:423.
6. Cyprian, 5:423.

insist on, namely, that if God is your Father, then the church must be your mother.

Joining with Cyprian's sentiments, John Calvin says, "I shall start, then, with the church, into whose bosom God is pleased to gather his sons, not only that they may be nourished by her help and ministry as long as they are infants and children, but also that they may be guided by her motherly care until they mature and at last reach the goal of faith . . . , so that, for those to whom he is Father the church may also be Mother."[7] A good mother nourishes and protects her children. The church (our "mother") has certain responsibilities toward God's children. But we also have responsibilities toward the church, one of which includes faithful attendance upon the means of grace to protect us from the attacks of the evil one, the world, and our sin. Backsliders usually lay the blame at the foot of the church, but many times such excuses are covers for hidden sins. So those who are given to a particular sin often decide to blame the church rather than repent and seek healing in the place where forgiveness of sins should be publicly proclaimed each Lord's Day in the elements of worship.

For Further Reflection

1. Why should corporate worship take precedence over private worship?
2. Does the church share some blame for people's leaving the church? If so, how?
3. How does the church start to lose priority in the Christian life? Why?
4. Read and meditate on Psalm 95; Hebrews 12:18–29.

---

7. John Calvin, *Institutes of the Christian Religion*, ed. John T. McNeill, trans. Ford Lewis Battles, 2 vols. (Philadelphia: Westminster Press, 1960), 4.1.1.

12

The Folly of Backsliding

Like a dog that returns to his vomit is a fool who repeats his folly.
(Prov. 26:11)

Do You Want to Go Away?

Jesus had to deal with temporary followers who "turned back and no longer walked with him" (John 6:66) when faced with hard teachings. In response to these so-called disciples' rejecting him, Jesus asked the Twelve: "Do you want to go away as well?" (v. 67). Peter wisely responded that there was no one else to go to, for Jesus, the Holy One of God, had the words of eternal life (vv. 68–69). Peter understood the folly of not following Christ, though later he would inexplicably suffer his own "turning away." His life shows us that any of us can be fully assured of the folly of forsaking Christ, only to do it later.

God's people have a sad history of turning from him, being chastised by him, crying out to him, and being restored by him (Ps. 85:1–9). In Psalm 85, we read of God's peace toward his people chastised for rebellion, but with a salient warning (v. 8): "but let them not turn back to folly." Samuel's moving words in his farewell address exhort the people and the king concerning this very folly: "Do not be afraid; you have done all this evil. Yet do not turn aside from following the LORD, but serve the LORD with all your heart. And do not turn aside after empty things that cannot profit or deliver, for they are empty" (1 Sam. 12:20–21). Ezra, too, acknowledges in his prayer that the evil that came upon the Lord's people was because of their "evil deeds" and "great guilt" (Ezra 9:13). Even so, God showed mercy in his punishments, prompting Ezra to pray: "shall we break your commandments again and intermarry with the peoples who practice these abominations?" (v. 14).

The Scriptures and Christian experience clearly teach us that God's rescue from patterns of sin and backsliding back to fellowship and joy in him gives no license to presume upon the grace of God. We should always remember not only the danger of returning to our sin, but also the folly of repeating past mistakes.

The fact of backsliding and apostasy in the Christian church cannot be ignored. Denying or ignoring them makes us worse than doctors who disregard obvious (and curable) diseases in their patients. Folly is a sin, and the worst folly is a gracious deliverance into the light followed by willing return to the darkness.

Don't Be Stupid

The love that God displays in delivering us from darkness to light came at a great cost: the death of his Son. The love of Christ was to him a great sacrifice, for there is no greater love than to lay down one's life for others (John 15:13). When we enter into and enjoy the love of God and then return to the world, we sinfully aggravate the triune God in a heightened manner.

We are like a man in a loving marriage who decides to pursue another woman. The unfaithful partner causes great and lifelong hurt for the offended one, even if there is forgiveness. God is always the offended and, beyond that, sinlessly innocent party; he can never be blamed in any way for our giving allegiance to another god. When we abandon him, we choose the offerings of a worthless idol over the goodness of the only true God. What folly!

When true children of God who possess the Spirit of Christ backslide, they will inevitably feel some intense bitterness sooner or later. At one time they had repented for their sin; the vomit of the soul had emerged, and they saw the horrors of sin. But now they are returning to that vomit in the hope that it can offer them some nourishment. When true Christians leave off communion with God, they will surely lose assurance; the peace they once enjoyed will grow cold. And they, like David, will have to pray, "Restore to me the joy of your salvation, and uphold me with a willing spirit" (Ps. 51:12). There can be no flowering of joy in the Christian life when the source of joy is ignored.

Thomas Goodwin wrote a powerful treatise on the folly of relapsing. He offers several compelling reasons to dissuade children of God from choosing the way of the world instead of the way of Christ. For example, he attests that if one sin gained a person the entire world, it would not be worth it: "no, not the loss of one hour's communion with God, which in a moment will bring you in more sweetness than all your sins can do to eternity. If all the pleasures of sin were contracted, and the quintessence of them strained into one cup, they would not afford so much as one drop of true peace with God does, being let fall into the heart."[1] Many young people leave the church—some having claimed conversion, perhaps truly—to seek out "better" things from the world: sex, parties, riches, and so forth. Yet their lack of an eternal perspective keeps them from seeing their foolish path when measured through the lenses of eternity.

---

1. Thomas Goodwin, *The Works of Thomas Goodwin*, 12 vols. (Edinburgh: James Nichol, 1861–66; repr., Grand Rapids: Reformation Heritage Books, 2006), 3:415.

The peace that God offers for those who walk with him, not against him, "surpasses all understanding" (Phil. 4:7). Paul's words about God's peace arise in the context of anxiety ("do not be anxious about anything," v. 6). So many young people today are riddled with anxiety, and instead of praying for God's peace, they turn for consolation and escape to such idols as alcohol, illicit drugs, video games, social media, sexual sin, and prescription medication. They turn away from God—and are they better off? Worldly pleasures are attached to the senses: the Lord's pleasures go beyond the senses; his peace surpasses understanding. God's "steadfast love is better than life" (Ps. 63:3). In connection with this truth, Goodwin asks: "If it were propounded to you, you must lose your life [in the] next moment if you should commit such a sin, would you venture [to do so], if you did believe [such a threat]? Now 'the loving-kindness of God is better than life,' and will you lose the enjoying of it, though but for a moment?"[2] Such treasures from the Lord are not worth tossing into the dumpster, only to retrieve from that very trash bin the fleeting pleasures of the world and its garbage. Thomas Boston, in his sermon "The Folly of Turning Aside from the Lord," challenges his readers, "I defy you to find out a substantial good for yourselves in the whole creation, separate from God."[3]

Once the garbage of the world is retrieved by the child of God walking in darkness, the delights of sin, from which Jesus saved the person, quickly lose their appeal. Without any saving knowledge of God, non-Christians find that some of the world's pleasures taste delicious for a while, but even unbelievers experience the diminishing returns of delight from sin, which promises but never gives lasting satisfaction. The once-tasty morsels of sin now need enhancement to remain pleasurable. An illicit magazine from

---

2. Goodwin, 3:415.

3. Thomas Boston, *The Whole Works of the Late Reverend and Learned Mr. Thomas Boston*, 12 vols. (Aberdeen: George and Robert King, 1851), 9:500.

the 1990s will have little impact on pornography addicts today, who "need" more and more crudeness from the porn industry to satisfy their appetite for destruction. When we truly experience God's grace, returning to those old "pleasures" will never bring the satisfaction that we once temporarily enjoyed. Even those in darkness know the emptiness of these worldly pleasures, but for the person who has experienced the light of Christ in his or her life, the delights of the world will never have a sweetness without some gall mixed in. This is a great mercy, by the way, from our Father, who never completely gives his children over to the world.

We should remember God's attitude toward us when we backslide. He is angry with the sins of those outside Christ, but for those who are in Christ yet walking in darkness, God is more grieved than angered. As Goodwin says: "To grieve him is more than to anger him. Mere anger [as] an affection can ease itself by revenge."[4] The Lord has loved us with the best and most costly love. Striving after and loving the world, in obedience to the flesh, "goes to his heart, grieves him rather than angers him," says Goodwin, "and such are the truest and deepest griefs."[5] There is a sense in which the aggravation of our sin, especially against knowledge of what is right and wrong, is far worse than before we knew the Lord. God does not experience in his divine essence a grief of pain, as if he were subject to passions, but such language of grief is used to highlight the evil of our sin toward God.

The child of God walking in the light senses deeply the wages for his or her sin: "death," namely, Christ's on the cross. But we also know the consequences of sin not only for the unrepentant in the life to come but for both them and the repentant in this life. David's life was fraught with difficulties and distresses after his psalm of repentance; he was washed, forgiven, and assured,

4. Goodwin, *Works*, 3:416.
5. Goodwin, 3:416.

but he would never be entirely free from the consequences of his actions. When we know that sin pays only with pain in the end, how can we be so stupid as to rush into it? "Satan promises the best but pays with the worst," warns Thomas Brooks; "he promises honor and pays with disgrace, he promises pleasure and pays with pain, he promises profit and pays with loss, he promises life and pays with death; but God pays as he promises, for all his payments are made in pure gold."[6] Count the cost, as Moses did, and look to God's reward (Heb. 11:24–26).

God's Mercies

God's love to his people has certain manifestations according to his wise and patient purposes. We are all justified by the same blood of Christ, yet he treats us in varying ways concerning our growth in grace. Goodwin makes the point that God "leaves some thus to sin after his love shed abroad in their hearts. Some he shews his free love unto, in keeping them from sinning; other, in pardoning them, and giving them repentance."[7] Most Christians experience all these realities at some point in their walk with the Lord. We are prevented by his grace and mercy from committing sins, sometimes not even fully aware of his gracious protection. But sometimes, for reasons that God alone knows, we are left to indulge in a pattern of sinning.

The example of Samson aptly reminds us of the folly of returning to sin, but also of God's mercies toward us despite our nonsense. Samson's faith receives honor in Hebrews 11, which is a testimony to God's grace. But the particulars are worth mentioning. Not unlike us in our sinful pursuits at times, Samson lusted for a Philistine wife against his parents' wishes

6. Thomas Brooks, *The Works of Thomas Brooks*, ed. Alexander B. Grosart, 6 vols. (1861–67; repr., Edinburgh: Banner of Truth, 2001), 2:322.
7. Goodwin, *Works*, 3:419.

and warnings and would not be refused (Judg. 14:1–3): "Get her for me, for she is right in my eyes" (v. 3; see also v. 7). In this instance, he did not care what was right in the Lord's eyes (see Deut. 6:18; Judg. 17:6; 21:25) and fell victim to his folly, betrayed by the very woman who was "right" and whom he had to have no matter what (Judg. 14:17–18). He did not learn, for he "went to Gaza, and there he saw a prostitute, and he went in to her" (16:1), knowing that the Gazites would seek to kill him (vv. 2–3). That he escaped does not undo his indiscretion. He then fell in love with Delilah, the third Philistine woman who would seduce him, and he would die because of this entanglement (vv. 4–30). He died in the Lord, with a heroic, Christlike act of faith, but it is also true that his folly cost him his life.

We must be careful about the example of Samson. We can glorify God for his mercy toward a man who acted foolishly but should have known better, since he was a judge (Judg. 15:20). To whom much is given, much is required (Luke 12:48). If we sin willfully and expect the same mercy as Samson, then we may as well also expect the ability to perform heroic acts of faith like Samson. You can't dismiss the graces evident in Samson's life and merely point to his vices, thinking that your own willful departures from the Lord into sin will be overlooked. Though a judge, Samson was judged by the Judge of all the earth. He felt the consequences of his sin (e.g., loss of his eyes). For Christians who consider romantic relationships with those outside the Lord (e.g., thinking, "I can be the instrument of their conversion"), they should imagine Samson as screaming down from the heavens, "Don't do it." God's mercies are not to be presumed upon. They are for the brokenhearted, not the hardhearted. To Samson's credit, he ended his race well, in faith. One could imagine him as praying the words of the tax collector, "God, be merciful to me, a sinner!" (Luke 18:13).

The point that must be delicately put is simple: God's mercy saved us from a meaningless life now and from future eternal judgment. That mercy we have received should keep us from returning to a life of folly and sin. But even if God's children do fall into a sustained pattern of sin and wander, there is still mercy for them. Yet this mercy will not remove all the consequences of our actions. Consequences remain, even for God's favorites. If they did for the man after God's own heart, they certainly will for you.

Application

In his *Treasury of David*, Charles Spurgeon speaks to the folly of backsliding in his comments on Psalm 85:8:

> Backsliders should study this verse with the utmost care, it will console them and yet warn them, draw them back to their allegiance, and at the same time inspire them with a wholesome fear of going further astray. To turn again to folly is worse than being foolish for once; it argues wilfulness and obstinacy, and it involves the soul in sevenfold sin. There is no fool like the man who will be a fool cost him what it may.[8]

This quote delightfully summarizes the main concern of this chapter related to those turning to a life of folly. We must resist the temptation to return to our former way of living. By God's grace, we know its utter bankruptcy, but the world, our sin, and the devil are relentless in their pursuit of our souls.

We must also face another regrettable fact of apostasy in relation to the folly of relapsing. True children of God, who have the Spirit of Christ dwelling in them, should ordinarily repent in this life of their folly of relapsing. But what of those who, to use Goodwin's words, "utterly fall away, and after they have been

8. Charles Spurgeon, *The Treasury of David: Containing an Original Exposition of the Book of Psalms*, vol. 4, *Psalm LXXIX to CIII* (London: Passmore & Alabaster, 1874), 87.

enlightened, and tasted of the good word of God, then fall again to the pleasures of sin, and never repent of them?"[9] These are the ones who return to their vomit (Prov. 26:11). But what can the world promise such souls? Can the world promise pleasures forevermore at the right hand of God (Ps. 16:11)?

Perseverance in the Christian life is not easy. Jesus knew this better than anyone else, and so continually emphasized it. Many believed in Jesus, but he did not "entrust himself to" or, perhaps, "believe in" them (John 2:24; "believed" and "entrust" in the Greek come from the verb *pisteuō*). When Jesus was with crowds, he spoke of self-denial as the hallmark of true discipleship. This involves daily taking up our cross and following Christ (Mark 8:34). If you try to save your life on your worldly terms, you will lose it all; but if you count it loss for Christ on his terms, you get it all back and more in the most glorious way possible (v. 35). Christ appeals to you in these hauntingly famous words: "For what does it profit a man to gain the whole world and forfeit his soul? For what can a man give in return for his soul?" (vv. 36–37). These rhetorical questions answer themselves, screaming, "Nothing! Nothing!" Boston asks you to count the cost: "Whatsoever you think you gain by turning aside from the Lord, a thousand times more is going to destruction in the meantime. Count what you give out, as well as what you get in, and you will soon see the gain worse than nothing" (see Matt. 16:26).[10]

This means, by way of final application, that our repentance should be frequent: daily acts of faith and repentance keeping our consciences sensitive to the guilt, danger, and horror of sin. When we stop repenting, we stop depending on God. We lose sight of his mercies and find ourselves wandering. Daily we must repent and ask God to lead us not into temptation (Matt. 6:12–13). Robert

9. Goodwin, *Works*, 3:428.
10. Boston, *Works*, 9:505.

Robinson understood something of our proclivity to wander in his well-known hymn, writing of the regenerate soul's desire for God to preserve us to the end:

> O to grace how great a debtor
> daily I'm constrained to be;
> let that grace now, like a fetter,
> bind my wand'ring heart to thee.
> Prone to wander—Lord, I feel it—
> prone to leave the God I love:
> here's my heart, O take and seal it,
> seal it for thy courts above.[11]

For Further Reflection

1. Why do we still feel drawn to the world? What keeps us from returning to worldliness?
2. What should we tell ourselves about love for the world versus love for God in terms of what each can offer?
3. What does recovery from backsliding teach us about God?
4. Read and meditate on Judges 16; Psalm 16.

---

11. Robert Robinson, "Come, Thou Fount of Every Blessing" (1758).

13

The Recovery of Backsliders

Among other acts of Christian communion, this is one of the chiefest, to restore those that are gone astray. (Thomas Manton)[1]

Our Charge Is Love

Andrew Fuller captures what I think should be the spirit of all who would write on the matter of backsliding: "Were it not for the hopes of being instrumental in saving some from the error of their way, and of inducing others to a greater degree of watchfulness, I should not have written the preceding pages. It can afford no satisfaction to expose the evil conduct of a fellow-sinner, or to trace its dangerous effects, unless it be with a view to his salvation or preservation."[2] As Paul said to Timothy, "The aim of our charge is love that issues from a pure heart and a good conscience and a sincere faith" (1 Tim. 1:5).

Any pastor paying attention to his flock and the universal church will face the harsh reality that God's people can get into a

---

1. Thomas Manton, *A Practical Commentary or Exposition on the General Epistle of James*, abr. and ed. the Rev. T. M. Macdonogh (London: W. H. Dalton, 1844), 396.
2. Andrew Fuller, *The Backslider* (London: Hamilton, Adams, and Co., 1840), 71.

lot of mischief. The fact of backsliding and its effects causes a great deal of anxiety among faithful pastors who care about the sheep (2 Cor. 11:28). Backsliding must be acknowledged, examined, and exposed. Yet in this process, there must also be a concerted effort to offer hope to backsliders, to provide a remedy, and to see God honored.

Our desire is simple: we wish for backsliders to return to praising God and living for him instead of themselves. Backsliders have not returned unless they return to praise and worship through repentance. The Christian life is not meant to be overcomplicated. God treats us as children, not as enemies that he wishes to confound. He also treats us according to his gracious, merciful, and patient nature. This provides the ground of all hope concerning the recovery of backsliders. But at the same time, God employs the gifts and graces of his servants to recover wandering sheep. Yet his servants must be just that—servants. Without such a commitment, we will want nothing to do with the often emotionally painful process of ministering to backsliders.

Means and Ends

Pastors and other godly people who share a concern for the spiritual well-being of the wayward can rest assured that if backsliders are true children of God, they will usually have some sensitivity to their spiritual malaise and wish to be delivered from it. Fuller claims that backsliders, "unless they be given up to a rejection of all religion," ordinarily wish to be restored, knowing their state to be unacceptable.[3] One of the scariest realities that pastors face is a person who is clearly not walking with the Lord, yet without awareness or care concerning his or her spiritual condition. That person may be an apostate rather than a backslider,

---

3. Fuller, 71.

though sometimes even the latter can be temporarily indifferent about spiritual matters.

We can and must exhort a brother or sister in the Lord when his or her spiritual slothfulness becomes clear and ongoing. Thomas Manton reminds us that besides the work of the ministers, "private Christians not only may, but must keep up a Christian communion among themselves. . . . They are mutually to stir up one another by speeches that tend to discover sin; to prevent hardness of heart and apostasy."[4] Our hope in such a holy confrontation may be more complex than we realize. Fundamentally, our hope is always in the Lord, who implants new life into a sinner. Yet he also gives us certain means to direct the godly in his way. For example, God gave David repentance after a time of darkness, but God also used Nathan to confront David. From this let us learn that while we hope and pray for God in victorious Spirit-energized grace to win over backslidden hearts, he does not want us to passively sit back and wait for some immediate work on the soul. Certainly, the Lord can and does at times perform such work, for example, through a crisis in the backslider's life or simply by the reading of God's Word. Still, he typically makes use of his servants to bring about these ends through means such as preaching, counseling, books, and personal dealings.

Our exhortations to backsliders must agree with the principles of God's Word if we expect his blessings. Casual indifference carelessly cries, "Peace, peace" to backsliders when there is no peace. But what is our basic approach to backsliders? We must realize that it is easier to drift away from the Lord than it is to return, just as it is easier to fall down a flight of concrete stairs than it is to climb back up, bruised, bleeding, and battered. Backsliders face a great battle in returning to the Lord, and those exhorting them should be prepared for all manner of emotions to arise from the

4. Manton, *Practical Commentary on James*, 396.

difficulty of the task. Manton wisely states that "error is touchy" and that often "conviction and reproof beget hatred."[5]

Still, few things are more rewarding in this life than being used by the Lord in his restoration of one backslider to joyful communion with the triune God. The world applauds a myriad of achievements by all sorts of people, but heaven applauds the faithful, courageous, patient, and gracious calling by Christ-honoring saints of backsliders back to the Lord.

Repentance and Praise

Richard Sibbes, in his remarkable yet largely unnoticed *The Returning Backslider*, published a series of sermons on Hosea 14, providing a thorough analysis of backsliders and how they can be restored to godly living.

Hosea 14 opens with a call to Israel to return to the Lord in repentance after stumbling in sin. Our great problem in this world, despite protestations to the contrary, is our sin. But as Sibbes notes, "all the power of the world, and of hell, cannot keep a man in misery, nor hinder him from comfort and happiness, if he will part with his sins by true and unfeigned repentance."[6] The prelude to this return must be a humble acknowledgment of one's sinful straying from the Lord. "I have this against you," argues Christ to the church of Ephesus, "that you have abandoned the love you had at first. Remember therefore from where you have fallen; repent, and do the works you did at first. If not, I will come to you and remove your lampstand from its place, unless you repent" (Rev. 2:4–5). Notice how restoration takes place: recognition, repentance, and renewed obedience—in that order.

As further evidence of the backslider's needed repentance,

---

5. Manton, 397.

6. Richard Sibbes, *The Complete Works of Richard Sibbes, D.D.*, 7 vols. (Edinburgh: James Nichol, 1863), 2:257.

Sibbes observes: "As we know, Manasseh, as soon as he put away sin, the Lord had mercy upon him, and turned his captivity, 2 Chron. 33:12, 13. So the people of Israel, in the Judges. Look how often they were humbled and returned to God, still he forgave them all their sins. As soon as they put away sin, God and they met again. So that, if we come to Christ by true repentance, neither sin nor punishment can cleave to us, Ps. 106:43, 44; 107:1, 9."[7] Just as we begin the Christian life with faith and repentance, so we continue in it daily with faith and repentance. Why should we pursue another plan for the backslider? Rolling up our sleeves and promising to do better without repentance is destined to hopeless and miserable failure.

John Owen highlights one of the important differences between a backslider and an apostate, namely, that apostates are not capable of repentance. "No man is past hopes of salvation until he is past all possibility of repentance," affirms Owen, "and no man is past all possibility of repentance until he be absolutely hardened against all gospel convictions."[8] What Owen calls "recoverable backsliding" makes repentance both possible and necessary, and therefore ought to be our first aim in restoring someone who has drifted away.

Confronting backsliders, especially those we love and with whom we have had sweet fellowship, requires courage, since repentance cannot be bypassed in the process of restoration. But the rewards are great if God grants repentance. Those who truly admit their sin and turn back from it to the Lord will necessarily possess a renewed appreciation for Christ's atoning work on behalf of sinners. Forgiven sin must arouse a renewed love for God. Likewise, the grace of forgiveness joins with the grace of transformation, with the expectation that the Spirit of holiness will subdue sin's power, since sanctification is a friend of justification (1 Cor. 1:30).

7. Sibbes, 2:257.
8. John Owen, *The Works of John Owen*, ed. W. H. Goold, 24 vols. (Edinburgh: T&T Clark, 1850–53), 7:236.

There is, then, a great encouragement for backsliders to go to their loving heavenly Father for forgiveness. He loves to honor his Son, and we do also when we make the best use of Christ's work for us. After we ask God, "Take away all iniquity," we can also plead that he "accept what is good" in terms of our renewed obedience (Hos. 14:2). We have hope that once we return we can do so well, making good progress again in Christlikeness, "bringing holiness to completion in the fear of God" (2 Cor. 7:1).

Praise should follow repentance: "O Lord, open my lips, and my mouth will declare your praise" (Ps. 51:15). If we meet with success in persuading a backslider to turn from sin back to the Lord, we cannot stop there. There must be praise and worship. They arise as we face our sin in the light of our Father's lovingkindness, mercy, and patience. When the backslider realizes how he or she has treated God with contempt, disregarded him without good cause, and made little to no use of his blessings, and yet finds that he is willing to receive the person into loving communion, the only appropriate response after repentance is praise. Praising God has a transformative power, for we become like what we worship. The Israelites were told, upon repentance, that God would heal them and "love them freely" (Hos. 14:4). He loves freely.

In the new covenant we have the clarity of Christ's person and work as the grounds for why God loves us freely. Octavius Winslow thus speaks of Christ's love in restoring the backslider: "Nothing but the most infinite, tender, unchanging love, could prompt him to such an act. There is so much of black ingratitude, so much of deep turpitude in the sin of a believer's departure from the Lord, that but for the nature of Christ's love, there could be no possible hope of his return."[9] We find that when a backslider returns to the Lord, it is the Lord's doing: "He restores my soul.

9. Octavius Winslow, *Personal Declension and Revival of Religion in the Soul* (Eugene, OR: Wipf and Stock, 2001), 261.

He leads me in paths of righteousness for his name's sake" (Ps. 23:3). John Bunyan captured this well in his allegory *The Holy War* (1682), in which Prince Emanuel, symbolic of Christ, addresses the backslidden-now-restored Town of Mansoul, symbolic of the individual soul and the corporate church, declaring, "The way of back-sliding was thine, but the way and means of thy recovery was mine."[10] As the Good Shepherd, Jesus not only saves and protects his sheep, but brings them back into the fold when they stray. He does this for his name's sake and our good. The restoration of wandering sheep occurs because Christ and the Father love us freely.

The parable of the prodigal son reveals the character of the Father toward a returning backslider. When the father saw his son returning, he "felt compassion, and ran and embraced him and kissed him" (Luke 15:20). The son, showing true repentance ("Father, I have sinned against heaven and before you," v. 21), was received into what Winslow calls "the most expressive of undiminished love, of yearning tenderness, of eagerness to welcome his return."[11] Like the lost sheep and coin, this parable is about the repentance of a lost sinner, whom the Father lovingly receives. Still, as the Father receives us with the open arms of love in our conversion, so too he does when we return to him from going off to the far country anew. There is a sense, then, that the return of the backslider bears significant likeness to the conversion of a sinner. In our exhortation to backsliders to repent and turn again to the Lord, we have failed miserably if we neglect to mention the promise of a heavenly celebration that ensues when a child of God returns home. God is not the older brother, though many backsliders, in their unbelief, treat God as though he were like him.

10. John Bunyan, *The Holy War, Made by King Shaddai upon Diabolus, for the Regaining of the Metropolis of the World; or, the Losing and Taking Again of the Town of Mansoul*, ed. Roger Sharrock and James F. Forrest (Oxford: Clarendon Press, 1980), 246.

11. Winslow, *Personal Declension*, 275.

Application

We will all be faced with a time in our lives when we or those we know and love backslide. In fact, many of us will likely find ourselves in both situations. We are bound by the commandment, "So whatever you wish that others would do to you, do also to them, for this is the Law and the Prophets" (Matt. 7:12). So would you want to be warned of your danger in such a situation?

Love has certain demands, some of which can be extremely costly. Most pastors will tell you of the pain and heartbreak they suffer when dealing with church members who have forsaken their first love. Our exhortations and calls to repentance and renewed faith in Christ, no matter how tenderly carried out, are not always well received. We may even find that backsliders not only deny their plight but also turn to attack us and then go off backstabbing us before others. Have you ever been the recipient of such behavior? So has Christ. Have you ever given it? Yet Christ freely forgives the repentant. Often, however, over time, the persons rebuked begin to see their sin and their hearts soften. They remember:

> Better is open rebuke
>   than hidden love.
> Faithful are the wounds of a friend;
>   profuse are the kisses of an enemy. (Prov. 27:5–6)

While we have a duty to be faithful to God's Word and apply it appropriately to the situation at hand, we must also remember that, like salvation, the "growth" is from the Lord (1 Cor. 3:6) as the work of the Spirit. So while we are God's instruments to bring the truth to drifters, repentance is God's gift to bring them back to shore.

When we cultivate close friendships with our brothers and sisters in Christ, we can then minister to them in their time of need. For example, ten years of close fellowship (through the good and bad times) provide an open door to speak truth to the erring saint who, because he or she knows you and your love, is willing to listen. Have you not found that those closest to you are best suited to lovingly confront you? Never underestimate, then, the value of cultivating relationships with others for such times. The recovery of backsliders is a complex process with simple solutions. As Richard Baxter says in *The Reformed Pastor*: "The whole course of our ministry must be carried on in a tender love to our people. We must let them see that nothing pleases us but what profits them. . . . We must remember that pastors are not lords but fathers and therefore must be affectionate to their people as to their own children."[12] If a pastor fails to show tender shepherd-love toward his people, he will have an exceedingly hard time winning them when he needs to. This also applies, in some measure, to all of us when addressing the sin of others. To the degree that you invest love, kindness, patience, and the like in the lives of others in the church, God can use you in the recovery of backsliders. When a backslidden Christian realizes your love and care, that person will be more likely to receive your words, even if they are difficult to hear.

In Galatians 6:1, Paul urges us as believers to be gentle when we seek to restore someone overcome by sin, and to be watchful lest we fall into the same temptation. You must come in humility and gentleness whether dealing with someone's specific sin (e.g., a father's outburst of anger) or pattern of life (e.g., an abusive backsliding father finally exposed). The fruit of the Spirit brings to us both the faithfulness to confront the sinner and the gentleness to approach that one. We cannot expect good results when we look down our noses at the backslider with a haughty, self-righteous spirit. Not just our words, but our manner must be Christlike, for

12. Richard Baxter, *The Reformed Pastor*, updated and abr. Tim Cooper (Wheaton, IL: Crossway, 2021), 66.

he is gentle with us beyond our comprehension. Manton reminds us that our faithful reproofs are not designed to "accuse and condemn, but to counsel and convert an erroneous person. . . . We must first endeavour to burn sinners in the fire of love."[13] Burning sinners in the fire of love! Indeed.

For Further Reflection

1. Have you ever had to talk to a backslider? What did you say?
2. Consider a backslider who sees the need to come back to church after two years of living for self. What will such a person's repentance look like, and what timing should we expect for results?
3. Have you ever had someone confront you harshly? Describe what that was like compared to a more gentle approach used by someone else.
4. Read and meditate on Psalm 23; Hosea 14; James 5:13–20.

13. Manton, *Practical Commentary on James*, 397.

14

The Slide to Apostasy

Solemn as this declaration [Heb. 6:4–6] is in itself, and alarming as it is to certain characters—there is nothing in it to discourage, or terrify, a humble child of God. (James Smith)[1]

Types of Apostasy

Reformed theology in general seeks to make sense of truths about the visible church and salvation in line with scriptural teaching. For example, we have very few differences concerning the perseverance of the saints. A true saint in Christ will persevere to the end. Many sermons have been preached and much writing has occurred on this doctrine. But another truth gets little such attention, and that is total apostasy—perhaps because we do not like to discuss it or the uncertainties that exist about when it occurs. When does a once-professing Christian, having enjoyed certain privileges and blessings and rejected them with Christ, become irrecoverable? When does it become impossible for a person to repent?

1. James Smith, *Sunny Subjects for All Seasons* (Halifax: Milner & Sowerby, 1858), 89.

To be clear, one may be called an apostate because of defection from the gospel, but he or she may in fact recover. Not all apostasies are equally heinous. Some people incur greater guilt and judgment because of the nature of their apostasy. Were they teachers in the church or laypersons? Do they quietly apostatize, or are they vigorous in their hatred of Christ's teaching? When we can reasonably answer such questions, we may solemnly conclude from Scripture that some apostates turn to such a dark place of being handed over to their sin, Satan, and the world. At this point, there remains no chance of true repentance; God has already judged them in this life.

In some sense, we all want to know the truth in these matters not only for ourselves but for those we love—perhaps those who have jumped the fence and run off into the far country away from Christ. In another sense, we do not want to discuss it or read about it because it makes our stomachs turn to think about someone's apostatizing. Yet we must remember that God has revealed truths concerning total apostasy for our good. We need to think on these matters and think rightly about them. For example, a backslider may wrongly conclude that he or she is hopelessly beyond recovery because the bar for total apostasy has been set quite low. But the biblical bar for irrecoverable apostasy remains quite high. This should give us great hope but without foolish presumption; apostasy remains a real and present danger. In this chapter, with the help of John Owen, we will scripturally examine the stages of apostasy with the goal of knowing when an apostate is beyond hope of restoration.

Impossibility

In the classic text on irrecoverable apostasy, the author of Hebrews attests in 6:4–6 that "it is impossible in the case of those who have once been enlightened, who have tasted the heavenly

gift, and have shared in the Holy Spirit, and have tasted the goodness of the word of God and the powers of the age to come, and
then have fallen away, to restore them again to repentance, since
they are crucifying once again the Son of God to their own harm
and holding him up to contempt." The word "impossible" (Greek,
adynaton) here as elsewhere in Hebrews carries a strong force: "it
is impossible for God to lie" (Heb. 6:18); "And without faith it is
impossible to please him" (11:6). In short, "impossible" in these
instances describes something that absolutely cannot happen.
The impossibility in our passage concerns certain people who
absolutely cannot be restored to repentance (6:6). These people
received true spiritual blessings from the Lord (e.g., they have
been enlightened), yet those do not lead to true saving union
with Christ. Not only do total apostates lose these blessings, but
the blessings become curses to them.

In chapter 3 ("The Varieties of Christians"), we considered
the nonelect's receiving the Holy Spirit in a certain sense, but not
savingly. These professors experienced the power of the gospel
in significant ways, but without regenerate hearts. For those in
Hebrews 6:4–6, the glorious blessings that they once enjoyed and
experienced they lost without losing salvation, since they never
had it to begin with. One of the reasons that these passages make
us uncomfortable is that they on the surface seem to say that we
can lose our salvation. Rather, within the context of the covenant
community, the visible gathered church, unregenerate members
of the body lose great blessings. Among such blessings is a kind of
superficial nonsaving repentance from sin and faith in Christ that
brought and kept them in the fold but now has been lost without
hope of restoration (Heb. 6:6). Their failing to truly close with
Christ means, according to God's sovereign purposes, that they
will not ever be savingly joined to Christ. Beyond this, they will
not ever be restored to even the state of spiritual blessings that
they once enjoyed.

Let's open this up some more with Owen's help. Real and internal repentance comes through the regenerating work of the Spirit as a saving grace. It cannot be lost, since it arises from a vital union with Christ. Hebrews 6:6 does not have such repentance in mind, "for no man can be renewed again unto that which he never had," according to Owen.[2] But there also exists a repentance that is "outward in the profession and pledge of it."[3] This "repentance" respects an outward profession of the faith in the context of the visible church, usually with the seal of baptism that spoke of many spiritual realities (e.g., washing of sins). Sadly, what was outwardly signified did not become an internal reality.

The question before us in this chapter concerns how we are to identify such persons so that we do not unwisely take Hebrews 6:4–6 and apply it to those of whom it does not speak.

Signs and Evidences

What, then, are the chief characteristics of the irrecoverable apostate? In Owen's work on apostasy, he offers several recognizable stages in the slide to total apostasy. It seems that one may be at an early stage and, by God's grace, be converted (for the first time) in true repentance. But there does come a point when that is no longer possible according to God's purposes. We now come to consider those stages beyond this point.

First, apostates, according to Owen, manifest the *"loss of all taste of any goodness or excellency in the gospel."*[4] Such people had once "tasted the goodness of the word of God" (Heb. 6:5), found many things agreeable to their hearts and souls, understood the basics of the gospel, and seen some loveliness in Christ's person and work.

2. John Owen, *The Works of John Owen*, ed. W. H. Goold, 24 vols. (Edinburgh: T&T Clark, 1850–53), 7:89.

3. Owen, 7:89.

4. Owen, 7:231.

Second, losing any taste in the excellency of the gospel is "quickly followed with *a loss of all prevailing evidence and conviction of the truth of the very doctrine of the gospel*."[5] Those truly united to Christ have from the Holy Spirit a conviction of biblical truth and his internal testimony of it. They may not understand all the mysteries of the faith, but they know that apart from Christ they are hopeless. Apostates, however, may have seemed to embrace the truth while yet lacking any conviction in their souls that it is life-saving truth. Thus, in apostatizing, they forsake their apparent yet superficial embrace of truth.

Third, apostates very often show contempt for the things promised in the gospel.[6] This is where the matter becomes exceedingly dangerous, since it appears to manifest the slide to total apostasy. At this point, truths such as the following are despised: free salvation through Christ's death and resurrection, the promise of heaven to the faithful in Christ, the hope of worshiping the triune God in glory, and (for some apostates) the hope of an afterlife altogether. Apostates may also reject the Christian idea of heaven and trade it for some undefined place of serenity that is open to all, except the very worst of humanity (e.g., Adolf Hitler, Joseph Stalin, and right-wing Christians). Christ always proves to be the stumbling block for apostates. "They will rather have any interest in God than have it by Christ," says Owen.[7]

Fourth, with Christ now rejected as the one who can alone offer eternal life, apostates *"choose some other way or means in the place and stead of Christ and the gospel, for the ends which they once sought after by them."*[8] Such people may keep an interest in a deity, even to the point of worship. With the seed of religion in their hearts, they replace Christian doctrine with something

5. Owen, 7:231.
6. Owen, 7:232.
7. Owen, 7:233.
8. Owen, 7:233.

(anything) man-made, with certain rules of life required and blessings (temporal or otherwise) of obedience promised. Apostates may also absolutely abandon not just Christ's way of salvation, but any view of God that requires something of them. Their "religion" turns to something else (e.g., transgender activism, atheistic environmentalism). They have no regard for any warnings that they once intellectually embraced as professing Christians. Their sins become shamelessly open, perhaps not only in practice but also in promotion: calling good evil and evil good (Isa. 5:20).

Fifth, apostates' open wantonness and promotion of wickedness often lead to hatred for the faithful whose words and lives testify against such ways.[9] As Owen notes, "great apostates have been always great persecutors, in word or deed, according to their power. As those who love Christ do love all that are his, because they are his, so they that hate him do hate all that are his, because they are his; and their hatred, because it is against the whole kind, acts itself every way possible."[10] These apostates know what Christians believe, even in the most humble, gracious manner, about the eternal destinies of all in the world and how apostates are under the judgment of God. Perhaps in the deep recesses of the apostates' hearts, they know their hopeless condition out of which arises a hatred toward Christ's people.

Sixth, apostates hate not only Christ's people, but also the Holy Spirit,[11] since he glorifies Christ in various ways, such as granting faith and holiness to the elect. In a later warning passage, the writer of Hebrews speaks of those who "go on sinning deliberately" (Heb. 10:26), have "trampled underfoot the Son of God," and have "outraged the Spirit of grace" (v. 29). Interestingly, once the works of the Spirit are derogated, apostasy becomes, argues

9. Owen, 7:233–34.
10. Owen, 7:234.
11. Owen, 7:234.

Owen, "formally irremissible."[12] So while the pattern from the beginning of apostasy is certainly serious, there does appear to be a point of no return.

Seventh, Owen attests: *"An open profession of a detestation of the gospel*, so far as it is consistent with their worldly interests and advantages, completes the soul-ruining sin we treat of."[13] At this point, apostates openly express their hatred of the Christian religion. In earlier stages, they may have thought similarly, but now their degeneracy has taken such a turn that they loudly proclaim their fury against Christ and his people. These apostates are irredeemable because God has given them over to a debased mind. Consider, for example, those raised in the church who not only have turned away from their profession but pursue academic careers with the express purpose of unleashing with fury their intellectual pursuits (e.g., historical or biblical studies) on the world via their teaching or writing careers. Their eternal judgment occurs, in a certain sense, before death as they spurn great light and blessings (Heb. 6:4–6) and heap upon themselves condemnation. Their judgment goes beyond even the inhabitants of Sodom or, argues Owen, the "generality of the Jews who crucified Jesus Christ in the days of his flesh."[14] Their blessings have become a curse.

Application

Perhaps someone you know (or you yourself?) has walked very far from that person's original profession and wonders whether he or she falls under the judgment of Hebrews 6:4–6. We cannot overstate the danger of walking contrary to the light to which we have been called. Yet we can be encouraged that backsliders

12. Owen, 7:234.
13. Owen, 7:234.
14. Owen, 7:235.

and even some temporary apostates are not beyond hope. Peter could deny Christ with "I do not know the man" (Matt. 26:72, 74) and be recovered, in opposition to Judas, who was remorseful without true repentance in his complete, irrecoverable betrayal of our Savior, as the most wicked apostate ever to live (27:3–4).

Some backsliding lasts months and years, involving many particular sins, of which all can be repented. In spite of the perilous danger surrounding such persons, they are not necessarily shut out of heaven. Owen offers this "safe rule in general," namely, "that he who is spiritually sensible of the evil of his backsliding is unquestionably in a recoverable condition; and some may be so who are not yet sensible thereof, so long as they are capable of being made so by convictions. No man is past hopes of salvation until he is past all possibility of repentance; and no man is past all possibility of repentance until he be absolutely hardened against all gospel convictions."[15] May we prayerfully cling to such a hope for our backsliding loved ones.

You may reach a point at which you have to leave the backsliders to themselves: "Do not give dogs what is holy, and do not throw your pearls before pigs, lest they trample them underfoot and turn to attack you" (Matt. 7:6). In the case of the gospel, we know that the message is to be taken to all and preached to all (28:18–20). Yet the context of this passage indicates that there comes a time when we need to move on. Jesus instructed the Twelve on one occasion, "And if anyone will not receive you or listen to your words, shake off the dust from your feet when you leave that house or town" (10:14). This applies not only to preaching (see Acts 18:5–7), but also to our personal dealings with others. You will at times need to move on from those obstinately hardened to your exhortations, as well as apostates who not only are deaf to pleas to repent but also actively oppose them and perhaps even you.

15. Owen, 7:236.

With all of this said, no one who wants to repent will be kept from receiving forgiveness. Irrecoverable apostates do not want to repent. They do not say, "I would love to turn to the Lord, but I simply can't because it is impossible." They are getting what they wish and will find a just and righteous Lord who gives it. Anyone who has even the slightest degree of remorse and asks whether there is hope of salvation may be restored. God is merciful and patient, yet also just and righteous. The person who wishes to turn to the Lord will find a gracious Savior. Let this person know it. Embrace this hope for yourself.

For Further Reflection

1. How does this view of apostasy agree with the doctrine of the perseverance of the saints and help to keep us from presumption?
2. How do John Owen's stages of apostasy agree with your personal observations of those who have denied the faith?
3. Is it true that there is always hope for all people while they live, without exception, or do the Bible in general and Hebrews 6 in particular teach something different?
4. Read and meditate on Nehemiah 9 (see especially vv. 19–21); Hebrews 6.

15

The Victory of Weak Grace

*Is it not a demonstration of great power, to keep a small spark of
fire that it shall not be quenched in a flood of water? Yet behold that
little spark of grace in you shall not be quenched in you by the flood
and torrent of your corruptions. It is by God's power that the least
measure of grace shall be preserved.* (Christopher Love)[1]

Winning Is Everything

Grace can be resisted, or it can be irresistible. Why? Because
grace can be understood in reference to common gifts or special
gifts. Common gifts pertain to both believers and hypocrites in
the church. For example, a man can be an awesome preacher
while being a hypocrite without Christ. Special gifts, however,
apply solely to those who possess the fruit of the Spirit (Gal.
5:22–23).

In *Precious Remedies against Satan's Devices,* Thomas Brooks
speaks of the differences between "renewing grace, and restraining

---

1. Christopher Love, *Grace: The Truth and Growth and Different Degrees
Thereof* [. . .] (London: T. R. and E. M., 1652), 33.

grace; between sanctifying grace, and temporary grace."[2] Distinguishing the various effects and purposes of grace helps us to understand the nature of backsliding and also apostasy. One of the main concerns of this book has been to distinguish backsliding yet true Christians from professing yet unregenerate Christians, the latter of whom either apostatize or remain in the visible church, yet remain in their sins and without saving union with Christ. In this chapter, we will focus not only on the differences between true believers and hypocrites, but also on how even the weakest (yet saving) grace will prove victorious in the end.

The phrase *weak grace* may sound odd to some. Writers in times past used it to distinguish between weaker and stronger Christians, the babes and mature in Christ (1 Cor. 3:1–15; Heb. 5:11–14). But while one should endeavor to be strong in the Lord, even the weak, who possess a spark of saving grace, are heirs of salvation.

True Grace

The one who possesses true grace has an inner and outward glory and beauty, which Christ desires (Ps. 45:11). Our graces of faith, hope, and love are from the hand of Christ, who loves seeing them in us. We are filled with glory: "All glorious is the princess in her chamber, with robes interwoven with gold" (v. 13). With this special grace from Christ, our understanding, will, and affections are glorious. As Brooks says, "it casts a general glory upon all the noble parts of the soul: and as it makes the inside glorious, so it makes the outside glorious."[3] "In many-colored robes" we are led to Christ (v. 14). Saving grace gives us true life: "A healthy tree cannot bear bad fruit, nor can a diseased tree bear good fruit.

2. Thomas Brooks, *Precious Remedies against Satan's Devices* [. . .] (Philadelphia: Jonathan Pounder, 1810), 197.
3. Brooks, 197–98.

Every tree that does not bear good fruit is cut down and thrown into the fire. Thus you will recognize them by their fruits" (Matt. 7:18–20).

But weak Christians desperately stand in need of the promise of what grace will do. Christopher Love wrote significantly on weak grace and argues that it possesses much value, for even if it "be little for the present, yet it will grow for the future to a greater measure."[4] Indeed, "little measure of grace once begun in the soul shall be perfected"; and the "weakest Christian has grace alike for quality, though not for quantity: though your grace be not so much; yet it is as true as others."[5] Our hope, then, is in what God has promised according to the power working in us.

Special grace gloriously acts as a fire "to burn up and consume the dross and filth of the soul" and as "an ornament to beautify and adorn it."[6] People who do not receive special grace remain who they are. In the animated movie *Beauty and the Beast*, once love entered the Beast's soul, he transformed into a prince. Without love, he remained a Beast. We are like this until the grace of God enters our souls and inwardly transforms and beautifies us.

Since special grace makes all things new in the inner man, it enables us to "perform spiritual actions with real pleasure and delight."[7] Sometimes living obediently by faith can be painful and burdensome to our souls because of indwelling sin, but we must also affirm that the Spirit powerfully gives us delight for the things of God, allowing us to join with the psalmists in saying:

But his delight is in the law of the LORD,
and on his law he meditates day and night. (Ps. 1:2)

4. Love, *Grace*, 40.
5. Love, 41.
6. Brooks, *Precious Remedies against Satan's Devices*, 198.
7. Brooks, 199.

Praise the LORD!
Blessed is the man who fears the LORD,
>   who greatly delights in his commandments! (Ps. 112:1)

Lead me in the path of your commandments,
>   for I delight in it. (Ps. 119:35; see also vv. 47, 92)

Loving God and obeying his commandments with delight do not truly occur in the unregenerate without the Spirit of Christ in their hearts. They may experience emotions in worship or derive enjoyment out of performing some act of service, but for them the Christian life in general is dull and full of drudgery. Such people think of getting their Christian duty in until they get to heaven while they longingly gaze over the fence into the delights and approval of the world. For those with special grace, we can affirm, Christ is in us because he is for us. We can therefore examine our hearts without fear of condemnation:

Search me, O God, and know my heart!
>   Try me and know my thoughts!
And see if there be any grievous way in me,
>   and lead me in the way everlasting! (Ps. 139:23–24)

Some today seem to think of this as unwanted introspection, but the psalmist clearly desires that we be directed in God's ways more fully and forever. Hypocrites, in contrast, are great at searching the hearts of others, while they observe, judge, slander, gossip, mock, and ridicule others and their graces that the critic knows nothing of.

Special grace gives us ability that the natural man never possesses. Brooks testifies, for example, that true grace enables us to "step over the world's crown, and take up Christ's cross; to prefer the cross of Christ above the glory of this world" (see Heb. 11).[8] Nothing can explain the choices of saints such as Joseph, Moses, Esther, and Daniel other than the special grace that radically alters our thoughts, affections, and decisions with a view to Christ's honor and glory. "Temporary grace," says Brooks, "cannot make the soul prefer Christ's cross above the world's crown: for when these two meet, a temporary Christian will step over Christ's cross, to take up, and keep the world's crown"[9] (see 2 Tim. 4:10 concerning Demas).

Ultimately, special grace gives the regenerate Christian a holy hatred of sin and a holy love of Christ. Christ and sin are opposites; grace gives us the preference of the former over the latter. Without special grace, sin wins in the end. With even the weakest special grace, love for Christ as our chief good will prove victorious. As Brooks attests: "In having nothing I have all things, because I have Christ; having therefore all things in him, I seek no other reward, for he is the universal reward. Nothing is sweet to me without the enjoyment of Christ in it; neither honours, riches, nor the smiles of creatures are sweet to me, and farther than I see and taste Christ in them. The confluence of all outward good cannot make a heaven of glory in my soul, if Christ, who is the top of my glory be absent."[10] Special grace, then, leads to a special end: a soul's satisfaction in and longing for the glory of Christ.

Weak Grace Victorious

Stephen Charnock, well known for *The Existence and Attributes of God*, also wrote on weak grace and how it will preserve and prove victorious. Christopher Love comforts with the affirmation that "the least measure of grace is enough to bring you to heaven."[11]

---

8. Brooks, 201.
9. Brooks, 201.
10. Brooks, 206–7.
11. Love, *Grace*, 42.

Charnock basically writes a whole book on that proposition. His treatment focuses not only on the attributes of God but also on the peculiar works of the Father, Son, and Holy Spirit in saving a child of God. It would be a full-length book today in its own right and remains one of the best treatments on assurance of salvation. When the seed of saving grace enters the soul, argues Charnock, "though mixed with a mass of corruption, . . . there will be victory, for as the weakness of God is stronger than men, so is the weakness of grace stronger than sin."[12] In special grace, God is the ally.

One chosen by the Father to life in Christ can never lose that life, since God's purposes can never be overruled by man's purposes. The final apostasy of a regenerate person is, according to Charnock, "against the whole tenor of the covenant of grace, against the attributes of God engaged in it and about it, against the design of Christ, the mediator of it, against the charge committed to him, against the ends of the Spirit's mission and abiding with us."[13] One attacking the doctrine of the perseverance of the saints attacks God. "A regenerate man, endued with this vital principle," says Charnock, "neither can nor will, by reason of this implanted inworking of the Spirit, fall from faith and serve sin, so as to give himself up wholly to the commands of it."[14] Interestingly, Charnock here not only opposes those who argue that a true believer can fall away even with special grace, but also highlights that Satan once believed this (see Job 1:8–11), "though he has since discovered himself more orthodox."[15] Satan may indeed know that true saints persevere to the end, but he likely does not possess infallible knowledge of who truly belongs to Christ, so he relentlessly attacks all in the hope of causing them destruction (1 Peter 5:8).

12. Stephen Charnock, *The Complete Works of Stephen Charnock*, 5 vols. (Edinburgh: James Nichol, 1864–66; repr., Edinburgh: Banner of Truth, 1985), 5:226–27.

13. Charnock, 5:254.

14. Charnock, 5:254.

15. Charnock, 5:254.

Charnock expresses, with wonderful pastoral insight and care, a deeply realistic picture of the Christian life:

> The vigour of our gracious actions is often enfeebled by the power of the flesh, that we do many times the evil we hate, and omit that good we love. And we cannot deny but that our acts flow [more] often from a corrupt than a renewed principle; yea, and those actions which flow from grace are so tinctured with the vapours of the other [sinful] principle, that they seem to partake more of the impressions of the law of sin than of the law of the [spirit]; so that our perseverance is not to be measured by the constant temper of our actions, but from the permanency of the habit. The acts of grace may be suspended by the prevalence of some sinful distemper, as the operations of natural life are in an epileptic.[16]

The act-habit distinction used above shows that even though we often act contrary to our new nature and identity, we nevertheless possess the habit of grace. Acts (sins) may take place, righteousness may wane for a time, but the habit of grace will never disappear.

Acts of sin bring with them the loss of the comfort we usually possess from the habit of grace present. A believer can lose the sense of God's favor without losing the substance. Acts of sin affect communion with God, but union cannot be lost. Union cannot be lost because the relation we have as sons of God is irrevocable. Crying to God as Father is a Spirit-wrought grace (Rom. 8:14–16). And so we are treated as children. Charnock anticipates an objection to the truth of an unbroken relationship between Father and son. What if a believer "disinherits" himself by disobedient living? A person cannot lose sonship unless he or she ceases to

16. Charnock, 5:255.

be a human, since nothing can separate us from the love of God: "For I am sure that neither death nor life, nor angels nor rulers, nor things present nor things to come, nor powers, nor height nor depth, nor anything else in all creation, will be able to separate us from the love of God in Christ Jesus our Lord" (vv. 38–39). Weak grace perseveres because, despite being weak, it is still given freely by God through an omnipotently strong promise.

The habit of grace enables life in relation to God as Father, through Christ, by the Spirit, and so cannot be lost. When Peter testifies that we have been "born again, not of perishable seed but of imperishable," he highlights the incorruptible nature and effects of our birth from above. Charnock reinforces such a thought, noting that "the blood of Christ does not purchase a corruptible redemption, so neither does the grace of Christ work a corruptible regeneration."[17] With David to encourage us, Charnock maintains that despite his gross fall, "we find him not praying for salvation, but the joy of it. . . . And also for greater degrees of sanctification, and cleansing his heart from its filthiness and falseness. Grace may indeed, like the sun, be under an eclipse, but its internal light and heat cannot expire."[18]

Grace, while a gift from God, can be "oppressed" or "over-topped" by sin like a fountain obscured by a flood. Yet once the flood subsides, the fountain bubbles up again in clear sight. It never stopped working, but was concealed by the floodwaters. Grace, like that fountain, will always bubble up and rise again, though obscured by sin for a time. This occurs because of our indissoluble union with the Fountain of Life, Jesus Christ. His eternal and immeasurable reservoir of springs can fill innumerable people without any loss, so he will always provide for us streams of living water (John 4:10, 14).

17. Charnock, 5:256.
18. Charnock, 5:256.

Charnock adds: "Grace can never be so blown out, but there will be some smoke, some spark, whereby it may be re-kindled. The smoking snuff of Peter's grace was lighted again by a sudden look of his Master. Yea, it may, by a secret influence of the Spirit, gather strength to act more vigorously after its emerging from under the present oppression, like the sun, more warm in its beams after it hath been obscured by fogs. Peter's love was more vigorous after his recovery."[19] Backsliders desperately need such encouragement even in the midst of the warnings essential to their souls. God can bring us back, but back to better than before; he can make us stronger; he can bring us into closer communion with him than we had experienced before. Weak grace proves victorious not only in bringing us home to our Lord, but also in making us stronger in him after our failings.

Application

When a young person asks me about a potential spouse, the thing that matters the most is whether the grace of God is in that person. This does not trivialize such matters as humor, intellectual pursuits, physical attraction, manners, personality, habits, and shared interests in various matters. But these things pale in comparison to spiritual matters and specifically whether that person belongs to the Lord and lives in his grace. If so, with a life displaying such sonship, the person's grace, even if weak, will persevere and end in victory. Along the way there will certainly be bumps, but there will also be glories.

The special grace in us as true saints leads us to truly hate sin, not just the consequences but also the remaining presence of it. Christ has given a deathblow to sin and to Satan in our hearts. Still, you know well that though defeated, sin dies a "lingering

19. Charnock, 5:256–57.

death" in our lives. So do not be surprised; you will have eruptions of sin in your life. But the habit of grace in you, if you are a true believer of even the weakest grace, is stronger than your sin. Grace in you means Christ in you, and he will win the victory. We are "strengthened with power through [God's] Spirit in [our] inner being" (Eph. 3:16) because Christ dwells in our hearts through faith (v. 17). The question whether weak grace will be victorious depends on whether Christ was triumphant through the cross and in his resurrection, ascension, and enthronement. If the latter is true, then so must the former be. Christ cannot lose, which means that the grace of God given to us from the hand of Christ will be victorious, despite our stumbling.

If you believe yourself to be a Christian "weak in grace," you should desire to be stronger. Never conclude, "Hey, even the weakest grace is true grace and wins in the end, so I'm good." Indeed, the weakest grace is true and will be victorious. Yet true grace should also lead you to conclude that you stand in need of more and more and more. Do not give up asking God, then, for that very "more" that he alone can offer. So it's not suitable for you to be "just fine" in your current state. Christopher Love has advice for you in such a state: "though you shall have the fruit of your grace when you die, yet you will want the comfort of your grace while you live. It is strength of grace that gives assurance. Weak grace will bring your soul to heaven, but it is the strength of grace [that] will bring heaven into your soul."[20] Those who have tasted that the Lord is good should want to taste more of such goodness. Don't be content with little when a lot is promised.

Brothers and sisters, let us never deny the victory of even the weakest grace, lest we unwittingly deny God, his promises, and his glory. Charnock encourages us along these very lines:

20. Love, *Grace*, 52.

Though it be possible and probable, and I may say certain, that the habit of grace in a renewed man, considered abstractedly in itself without God's powerful assistance, would fall, and be overwhelmed by the batteries of Satan and secret treacheries of the flesh, yet it is impossible it should wholly fall, being supported by God's truth in his covenant, his power in the performance, held up by the intercession of Christ, and maintained by the inhabitation of the Spirit. Our wills are mutable, but God's promise unchangeable; our strength is feeble, God's power insuperable; our prayers impotent, Christ's intercessions prevalent. Our sins do meritoriously expel it, but the grace of God through the merit of Christ doth efficiently preserve it.[21]

Amen. Our sins may be strong, but God is infinitely stronger; and if he is for us, who can be against us (Rom. 8:31)? He loves us freely (Hos. 14:4).

For Further Reflection

1. What is the value in distinguishing between general grace and special grace when you consider people both outside and inside the church?
2. How does Christ's identification with the "bruised reed" and "smoldering wick" (Matt. 12:20) relate to this chapter?
3. How can we be stronger in grace if it is a gift?
4. Read and meditate on Psalm 119:33–48; Romans 8:1–39.

21. Charnock, *Works*, 5:262.

Conclusion

In North America, and especially the United States, we are drawn toward positivity (unless using Twitter). Growing up with British parents, and having traveled the world extensively, but living most of my life in North America, I have dealt with somewhat conflicting ways of looking at life. Often, when a British person likes you, he or she has a unique way of showing affection in the form of saying something negative. (We call it *banter*.) Few countries and cultures quite emphasize positive thinking like Americans. This is not a criticism, for many great accomplishments and results arise from positive thinking.

In Christian circles, books such as *Your Best Life Now* by Joel Osteen and *The Purpose Driven Life* by Rick Warren have not lacked a willing readership. If "positive" sells, then why write a book with an apparently "negative" title: *The Pilgrim's Regress*?

As a pastor, I must deal with reality, not make-believe. And pastors face harsh realities, one of which is backsliding among the people of God, which sometimes manifests itself in open apostasy. We can ignore the issue, but that will solve nothing. We can dance around the issue, but only a rigorous exposé and analysis of backsliding, along with ways to defeat it, will yield lasting fruit. For that reason, this book has attempted to not only highlight the problems of backsliding and apostasy, but also offer solutions to either keep one from backsliding or cure one who is backsliding. In this case, preventive medicine will be easier to digest than restorative medicine, but praise God, there is a cure.

Bunyan's *The Pilgrim's Progress* is a master class in understanding the nature of the Christian life. Sure, one can query why Christian's burden wasn't dealt with sooner, but overall the book shares insights into the struggles of a Christian in this world in a way that has captured the hearts of perhaps millions of God's people. Its deeply realistic picture of the manifold dangers and temptations that believers face helps us to understand why backsliding happens: we have a lot of enemies, even one within (indwelling sin).

While we believe that we are freely saved by God's grace as we receive and rest upon Christ alone as he is offered in the gospel, we also believe that the life of faith is not easy. The Scriptures present to us these two realities. Both God's preservation and our perseverance are true: we persevere because God preserves. But the way we persevere, and the way God preserves us, is filled with mystery. He sometimes allows his children to backslide. He also allows hypocrites into the church—those who make an outward profession of faith and sometimes in this life openly renounce their former profession. We can't always understand why true Christians backslide or why apostates come so close yet remain so far from Christ. But despite these painful realities, we need to be equipped, with God's armor, to fight the good fight and make use of all the promises, blessings, and graces that we have received in Christ if we are going to make it to the Celestial City. And faithful shepherds need to be ever vigilant in watching over the flock to see whether any are wandering from the fold.

So while the title of this book is "negative," I trust that the book is far from it. The goal and aim in the pages you have read has been to help all of God's children who struggle in this world with remaining indwelling sin to safely arrive, despite many battle scars, to the place where they will behold the glory of God in the face of Jesus Christ by sight. Grace prepares us for glory, and faith prepares us for sight.

In the introduction, I quoted Octavius Winslow:

> If there is one consideration more humbling than another to a spiritually-minded believer, it is, that, after all God has done for him,—after all the rich displays of his grace, the patience and tenderness of his instructions, . . . the tokens of love received, and the lessons of experience learned, there should still exist in the heart a principle, the tendency of which is to secret, perpetual, and alarming departure from God.[1]

True. But if there is another consideration more humbling than another to us, it is that after all that God has done for us, he will continue to do more for us to make sure that his children, despite their departures in this life, will never be snatched out of his hand. Those warmed by this thought cannot, I believe, doubt the victory of grace, even in the weakest believer, who is saved by one who is infinitely strong.

---

1. Octavius Winslow, *Personal Declension and Revival of Religion in the Soul* (Eugene, OR: Wipf and Stock, 2001), 9.

For Further Reading

Readers interested in this topic can look carefully at the footnotes if they saw a topic addressed and referenced about which they would like to read more. That said, if I were to offer some suggestions based on my own research, I would ask you to consider the following.

The best overall work I came across was that by Octavius Winslow, *Personal Declension and Revival of Religion in the Soul* (Eugene, OR: Wipf and Stock, 2001). He is an underrated theologian, whose writing style and incisiveness of thought were particularly illuminating to me.

Thomas Watson's *The Doctrine of Repentance*, Puritan Paperback ed. (Edinburgh: Banner of Truth, 1998), is a good book on sin, but also a work on how to escape the ravages of sin through repentance. Like his other writings, it is clear, vivid, and theologically rich.

I would say that John Owen's *Overcoming Sin and Temptation*, ed. Kelly M. Kapic and Justin Taylor (Wheaton, IL: Crossway, 2015), is required reading on sin and dealing successfully with that evil of evils. The editorial work on this volume is quite good. I suggest purchasing *Apostasy from the Gospel*, vol. 14 of *The Complete Works of John Owen*, ed. Joel R. Beeke (Wheaton, IL: Crossway, 2022), which contains three of Owen's works: *Of the Mortification of Sin in Believers, Of Temptation: The Nature and Power of It*, and *The Nature, Power, Deceit, and Prevalency of Indwelling Sin.* The introduction by Joel Beeke and editorial work are first-class. Owen's exposition of Romans 8:13 in his work on mortification is well known, but his work on indwelling sin is probably more important, in my opinion.

Andrew Fuller, *Backslider* (n.p.: H&E Publishing, 2019), with a foreword by Michael Haykin, is another work full of pastoral wisdom and insight. It is not too difficult to read, either.

Naturally, one should be most familiar with John Bunyan's justly famous work, *The Pilgrim's Progress*. Some dare to criticize this work, but its insight into the true nature of the Christian life is almost unparalleled since the seventeenth century.

Lots of sections in various books require some digging. As noted above, you can follow the footnotes. But, dear reader, never forget that for all the gold found in some of the aforementioned volumes, these are only aids to your progress. These works are not indispensable compared to the reading of God's Word and prayer alongside it.

Bibliography

Adams, Thomas. *An Exposition upon the Second Epistle General of St. Peter.* London: Henry G. Bohn, 1848.

Alexander, Archibald. *Thoughts on Religious Experience.* Philadelphia: Presbyterian Board of Publication, 1841.

Ames, William. *The Marrow of Theology.* Edited and translated by John Dykstra Eusden. 1968. Reprint, Grand Rapids: Baker, 1997.

Anderson, A. A. *The Book of Psalms.* Vol. 2, *Psalms 73–150.* New Century Bible Commentary. Grand Rapids: Eerdmans, 1992.

Anselm. *Proslogion.* In *Eerdmans' Book of Christian Classics: A Treasury of Christian Writings through the Centuries,* 27–43. Grand Rapids: Eerdmans, 1985.

Augustine. *The City of God.* Translated by Marcus Dods. Loschberg, Germany: Jazzybee Verlag, 2015.

———. "Homilies on the First Epistle of John." In *Nicene and Post-Nicene Fathers,* edited by Philip Schaff, 7:501–5. Grand Rapids: Eerdmans, 1956.

———. *On the Spirit and the Letter.* Translated by W. J. Sparrow-Simpson. London: Society for Promoting Christian Knowledge, 1925.

Ball, John. *A Treatise of Faith* [. . .]. London: For Edward Brewster, 1657.

Bates, William. *The Whole Works of the Rev. William Bates*. 4 vols. London: For James Black, 1815.

Baxter, Richard. *The Reformed Pastor* [. . .]. London: James Nisbet & Co., 1860.

———. *The Reformed Pastor*. Updated and abridged by Tim Cooper. Wheaton, IL: Crossway, 2021.

Boston, Thomas. *The Whole Works of the Late Reverend and Learned Mr. Thomas Boston*. 12 vols. Aberdeen: George and Robert King, 1851.

Bridges, Jerry. *The Joy of Fearing God*. Colorado Springs: WaterBrook Press, 2009.

Brooks, Thomas. *Precious Remedies against Satan's Devices* [. . .]. Philadelphia: Jonathan Pounder, 1810.

———. *The Works of Thomas Brooks*. Edited by Alexander B. Grosart. 6 vols. 1861–67. Reprint, Edinburgh: Banner of Truth, 2001.

Bunyan, John. *The Fear of God*. London: Religious Tract Society, 1839.

———. *The Holy War, Made by King Shaddai upon Diabolus, for the Regaining of the Metropolis of the World; or, the Losing and Taking Again of the Town of Mansoul*. Edited by Roger Sharrock and James F. Forrest. Oxford: Clarendon Press, 1980.

———. "Mr. Bunyan's Last Sermon." In *The Select Works of John Bunyan* [. . .], 772–75. Glasgow, Edinburgh, and London: William Collins, Sons, and Company, 1866.

———. *The Pilgrim's Progress*. Edited by J. B. Wharey and Roger Sharrock. Oxford: Clarendon Press, 1960.

———. *The Works of That Eminent Servant of Christ, John Bunyan* [. . .]. 3 vols. New Haven, CT: Nathan Whiting, 1830.

Calvin, John. *Institutes of the Christian Religion*. Edited by John T. McNeill. Translated by Ford Lewis Battles. 2 vols. Philadelphia: Westminster Press, 1960.

Carson, D. A. *For the Love of God: A Daily Companion for Discovering the Riches of God's Word*. Vol. 2. Wheaton, IL: Crossway, 2006.

Charnock, Stephen. *The Complete Works of Stephen Charnock*. 5 vols. Edinburgh: James Nichol, 1864–66. Reprint, Edinburgh: Banner of Truth, 1985.

Clarkson, David. *The Practical Works of David Clarkson*. 3 vols. Edinburgh: James Nichol, 1865.

Cyprian. *Treatise on the Unity of the Church*. In *The Ante-Nicene Fathers*, edited by Alexander Roberts and James Donaldson, 5:421–29. New York: Charles Scribner's Sons, 1908.

DeYoung, Rebecca Konyndyk. *Glittering Vices: A New Look at the Seven Deadly Sins and Their Remedies*. 2nd ed. Grand Rapids: Brazos Press, 2020.

———. *Vainglory: The Forgotten Vice*. Grand Rapids: Eerdmans, 2014.

Edwards, Jonathan. *Charity and Its Fruits*. Edited by Tryon Edwards. Philadelphia: Presbyterian Board of Publication, 1874.

———. *The Works of President Edwards*. 4 vols. New York: Leavitt & Allen, 1856.

Erskine, Ebenezer. *The Whole Works of the Rev. Ebenezer Erskine: Consisting of Sermons and Discourses on Important and Interesting Subjects* [. . .]. 3 vols. London: William Baynes and Son, 1826.

Ferguson, Sinclair. "Apostasy and How It Happens." March 14, 2023. https://www.ligonier.org/learn/articles/apostasy-and -how-it-happens.

———. *The Christian Life: A Doctrinal Introduction*. Edinburgh: Banner of Truth, 1981.

Flavel, John. *The Works of the Rev. Mr. John Flavel*. 6 vols. 1820. Reprint, Edinburgh: Banner of Truth, 1997.

Fuller, Andrew. *The Backslider*. London: Hamilton, Adams, and Co., 1840.

———. *Backslider*. N.p.: H&E Publishing, 2019. With a foreword by Michael A. G. Haykin.

Goodwin, Thomas. *The Works of Thomas Goodwin*. 12 vols. Edinburgh: James Nichol, 1861–66. Reprint, Grand Rapids: Reformation Heritage Books, 2006.

Gouge, William. *A Commentary on the Whole Epistle to the Hebrews* [. . .]. Vol. 2. Edinburgh: James Nichol, 1866.

Henry, Matthew. *An Exposition of the Several Epistles Contained in the New Testament* [. . .]. London: John Clark, 1721.

Houston, James M. *I Believe in the Creator*. Grand Rapids: Eerdmans, 1980.

James, John Angell. *The Christian Father's Present to His Children*. New York: R. Carter, 1853.

Kierkegaard, Søren. *For Self-Examination / Judge for Yourself!* Edited and translated by Howard V. Hong and Edna H. Hong. Princeton, NJ: Princeton University Press, 2015.

Lloyd-Jones, D. Martyn. *Studies in the Sermon on the Mount*. Nottingham, England: Inter-Varsity Press, 1976.

Lombard, Peter. *The Sentences*. Bk. 3, *On the Incarnation of the Word*. Translated by Giulio Silano. Mediaeval Sources in Translation 45. Toronto: Pontifical Institute of Mediaeval Studies, 2010.

Love, Christopher. *Grace: The Truth and Growth and Different Degrees Thereof* [. . .]. London: T. R. and E. M., 1652.

Manton, Thomas. *The Complete Works of Thomas Manton*. 22 vols. London: James Nisbet & Co., 1872.

———. *A Practical Commentary or Exposition on the General Epistle of James*. Abridged and edited by the Rev. T. M. Macdonogh. London: W. H. Dalton, 1844.

Murray, John. *The Epistle to the Romans*. Grand Rapids: Eerdmans, 1997.

———. *Principles of Conduct: Aspects of Biblical Conduct*. Grand Rapids: Eerdmans, 1971.

Newton, John. *The Works of John Newton*. 4 vols. New Haven, CT: Nathan Whiting, 1824.

Owen, John. *Apostasy from the Gospel*. Vol. 14 of *The Complete Works of John Owen*. Edited by Joel R. Beeke. Wheaton, IL: Crossway, 2022.

———. *Overcoming Sin and Temptation*. Edited by Kelly M. Kapic and Justin Taylor. Wheaton, IL: Crossway, 2015.

———. *The Works of John Owen*. Edited by W. H. Goold. 24 vols. Edinburgh: T&T Clark, 1850–53.

Plumer, William S. *Vital Godliness: A Treatise on Experimental and Practical Piety*. New York: American Tract Society, 1864.

Prideaux, John. *Ephesus Backsliding: Considered and Applied to These Times* [...]. Oxford: Leonard Lichfield, 1636.

Ryle, J. C. *A Call to Prayer*. Carlisle, PA: Banner of Truth, 2002.

———. *Practical Religion: Being Plain Papers on the Daily Duties, Experience, Dangers, and Privileges of Professing Christians*. London: Charles Murray, 1900.

Scougal, Henry. *Works of the Rev. Henry Scougal*. Glasgow: William Collins, 1830.

Sibbes, Richard. *The Complete Works of Richard Sibbes, D.D.* 7 vols. Edinburgh: James Nichol, 1863.

Smith, James. *Sunny Subjects for All Seasons*. Halifax: Milner & Sowerby, 1858.

Spurgeon, Charles. "Love: A Sermon." In *The New Park Street Pulpit*, 5:33–40. London: Passmore & Alabaster, 1894.

———. *The Metropolitan Tabernacle Pulpit: Sermons*. London: Passmore & Alabaster, 1871.

———. "The Sin of Unbelief: A Sermon Delivered on Sunday Morning, January 14, 1855." In *The New Park Street Pulpit Sermons*, 1:17–24. London: Passmore & Alabaster, 1855.

———. *The Treasury of David: Containing an Original Exposition of the Book of Psalms*. Vol. 4, *Psalm LXXIX to CIII*. London: Passmore & Alabaster, 1874.

Ursinus, Zacharias. *Commentary on the Heidelberg Catechism.* Grand Rapids: Eerdmans, 1956.

Watson, Thomas. *A Body of Practical Divinity* [. . .]. London: Thomas Parkhurst, 1692.

—————. *A Divine Cordial: Or, the Transcendent Priviledge of Those That Love God.* London, 1831.

—————. *The Doctrine of Repentance.* Puritan Paperback ed. Edinburgh: Banner of Truth, 1998.

Whyte, Alexander. *Lord, Teach Us to Pray: Sermons on Prayer.* Vancouver: Regent College Publishing, 1998.

Winslow, Octavius. *Personal Declension and Revival of Religion in the Soul.* Eugene, OR: Wipf and Stock, 2001.

Index of Scripture

Index of Subjects and Names

of the fear of God, 14, 41,
77–78, 80–89, 107, 154
of grace, 102
of justification by faith alone,
71
of the perseverance of the
saints, xvii, 4, 9, 72, 159,
167, 174
duty, 2, 11, 30, 45–46, 58, 80,
91–94, 109, 114–15, 156
spiritual, 4, 33, 91–92,
96–97

Edwards, Jonathan, 16–17, 55,
96–97, 115–16
elders, xv, 27, 30, 71
elect, the, 26–27, 29, 39, 70, 164
Ephesian believers, 20, 52
Ephesus, 8, 11, 67, 152
Erskine, Ebenezer, 3
eternity, 53, 141
Eve, 1, 41, 43, 69, 82
evil, 10–11, 15, 41–42, 45, 48,
57, 66, 84, 94, 140, 164,
166

faith, ix, 2–5, 11, 15–17, 20–21,
32, 34–36, 40, 43–45,
52–53, 84–88, 95–96,
152–53, 161–64, 170–71
life of, xviii, 4, 35, 41, 43–44,
47–48, 68–69, 124, 127,
147–48, 182–83

professed, 2, 5, 26–27
saving, 26–27, 34–36, 43–44
Father, the, 17–18, 47–48, 79–83,
110–12, 115–16, 130,
137–38, 143, 154–55,
174–76
fear, 41, 114, 146, 172
of God, 77–89, 107, 122, 126
fellowship, xiii, xx, 1, 11, 98, 116,
130, 132, 140, 153, 156
Ferguson, Sinclair, xvii, xxi, 73
Flavel, John, 3–4, 75
flesh, the, xviii, 15, 21, 42, 57–58,
61, 74, 84, 86, 91–92, 97,
101, 105, 134, 143, 165,
175, 179
folly, 121, 139–42, 144, 146
fools, 139, 146
foolishness, 44, 71, 82, 141,
145–46, 160
foreknowledge, 21
forgiveness, 6, 15, 87, 138, 140,
153–54, 156, 167
freedom, 37–38, 65, 96, 120, 137
fruit, 28, 30–34, 48, 95, 178
bearing, 2, 28, 30–34, 86, 97,
181
of Christ, 20
of righteousness, 97, 112
of the Spirit, 52–53, 95, 157,
169
Fuller, Andrew, xiii, xxi–xxii, 58,
149–50

heart, 22, 87
  of Christ, 14, 127
  of faith, 69–70, 79, 83, 93–94,
    97, 100–102, 156, 176–77
  hardened (unbelieving), 2, 4,
    8, 43–44, 57–59, 61–62,
    94, 131, 136, 151, 161–64,
    172
hell, 44, 86–87, 152
Henry, Matthew, 91
Hezekiah, 14, 73, 75
holiness, xiii, xviii, 14–15,
    37–38, 77–78, 80, 83, 92,
    96–97, 100–102, 109,
    114, 153–54, 164
Holy Spirit, the 13, 22, 37, 43,
    91–92, 108–10, 116, 123,
    137, 153, 156–57, 169,
    171–72, 174–79
  grieving, 4, 98–100
  living in, 41
  power of, 19–20
  receiving, 15–16, 31, 34–35,
    95–96, 79–80, 161
  resisting, 2, 99, 164
  sanctification by, 26
  share in, 30–31, 130, 160–161
  unity with, 27–32, 53–55
honor, xxi, 33–34, 54, 56, 78,
    100, 136, 144, 154, 173
hope, 16, 35, 59, 82–83, 89, 115,
    120, 127, 141, 170–71
  in Christ, 7, 85–86, 163

  in promise of God, 20–22,
    149–51
  of salvation, 11–12, 153–54,
    160–61, 166–67
Hosea, xxi, 7, 12, 31–32, 36, 152,
    158
hospitality, xx, 69
Houston, James, 82
humility, 65–66, 69, 74–75, 157
hymns, xxiii, 31, 116, 148
hypocrisy, xxi, 74, 133
hypocrites, 26–27, 115, 133,
    169–70, 172, 182

idolatry, xxi, 10, 66, 68, 76
indulgence, 39, 42
infidelity, xxi, 10, 48, 74
iniquity. *See* sin
Isaiah, 7, 18–19, 23, 76, 78, 99
Israel, xxi, 7, 32, 68, 70, 84, 122–
    23, 152–53

James, John Angell, 125, 128
Jeremiah, 6–7, 41, 51, 63, 68, 70,
    76, 79, 89, 123
Jesus Christ, 2–6, 28–31, 40–41,
    87–88, 129–30, 169–70,
    176–77, 182–83
  faith in, 33–34, 51–54,
    159–60
  his ascension, 178
  knowing, 79–81, 25–27,
    122–24, 126–27

unity, 20, 114
Ursinus, Zacharias, 27, 192

victory, 14, 96, 151, 169–70, 173
   of Christ, 2–3, 20, 177–78
   of grace, 38, 183
virtue, 16, 38, 44, 53, 74
vivification, 15, 95, 101

Warren, Rick, 181
Watson, Thomas, 14, 38, 55, 61,
   74, 80, 93, 102, 185, 192
Westminster Confession of
   Faith, 4, 9
Whyte, Alexander, 108
Winslow, Octavius, xiii, xix, 16,
   37, 40, 55–56, 83, 98,
   106–7, 109, 114–15,
   154–55, 183
wisdom, 17, 19, 70–71, 79, 114,
   120

works, 75, 152–55
   God doing in us, 15–16,
   80–81, 96–97, 164–65,
   173–74
   good, 22, 85, 92, 132
   lawless, 31
   of ministry, 30
worship, 26, 154, 163, 172
   community, 29
   corporate, xx–xxi, 53–55, 57,
   85–86, 122, 129–38
   elements of, 82–83, 136
   family, 126–27
   habits of, 71
   public, 4, 85–86, 130–33
wrath, 67
   of God, 78, 84, 98, 102

zeal, ix, xix, 2, 8, 22, 52, 56, 113,
   132, 135
Zion, 131

Also by Mark Jones

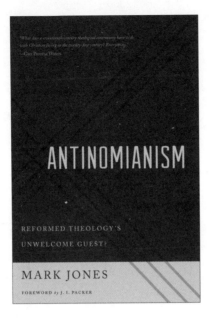

Hotly debated since the sixteenth century in the Reformed theological tradition, and still a burning issue today, antinomianism has a long and complicated story. This book is the first to examine it from a historical, exegetical, and systematic perspective. More than that, in it Mark Jones offers a key—a robust Reformed Christology with a strong emphasis on the Holy Spirit—and chapter by chapter uses it to unlock nine questions raised by the debates.

"The problem of antinomianism is a hardy perennial for the church. A mischievous movement is afoot at the moment—its soaring rhetoric about grace is matched by an equally casual presumption on grace. Mark Jones's book is thus to be welcomed: it is biblically grounded, historically sensitive, and above all timely."
—**Carl R. Trueman**, Author, *The Rise and Triumph of the Modern Self*

Did you find this book helpful?
Consider writing a review online.
We appreciate your feedback!

Or write to P&R at editorial@prpbooks.com
with your comments. We'd love to hear from you.